*family field guide*
— S E R I E S —

VOLUME TWO

# Rocky Mountain Plants

TREES . SHRUBS . WILDFLOWERS

*written by*
**Garrick Pfaffmann**

*illustrated by*
**Hilary Forsyth**

**BearBop Press** LLC

BASALT COLORADO USA

## family field guide
— SERIES —

## *field notes*

ISBN-13: 978-1-882426-26-3

Published by:

BearBop Press, LLC


Illustrated by:

Hilary Forsyth


Designed by:

words pictures colours graphic design


Distributed by:

WHO Press

www.whopress.com

*581.978*
*PFA*
*9/07*

Library of Congress Control Number: 2007925791

This book is not intended to encourage experimentation with plants as foods or any medicinal purposes. Neither the author nor the publisher may be held liable for any illness, injury or death caused by experimentation from any plants described in this book.

family field guide

# Acknowledgements

Thanks to the many people who lent a helpful and patient hand in helping to prepare this book. Special thanks to John and Lindsay for their patience and to Janis Huggins for her botanical expertise. Thanks also to Maria Armstrong, Anne Siewert, Kelly Alford and Warren Ohlrich for their writing, designing and publishing expertise, respectively. It is a blessing to be surrounded by so many talented people.

## Author's Dedication

To teachers, both formal and informal,
who demonstrate the value
of time spent drawing, comparing, understanding
and smelling the roses.

## Illustrator's Dedication

For all people, young and old,
who delight in noticing the small and
large surprises in living things,
which communicate with color,
shape and pattern,
instead of words and sounds.

# How To Use This Book

Sixty easy-to-identify plants have been selected as a basis for describing the roles and characteristics of plants within the Rocky Mountain region. Traditional field guides focus on plant identification and use language which requires a botanical dictionary to define botanical terms. Plant biology books, on the other hand, refer to generic plant characteristics and do not focus on a community of plants within arms reach of the reader. This book blends the traditional plant field guide with elementary plant biology allowing easy identification and understanding of plant adaptations, interactions, growing patterns, roles in ecosystems and more, all within the Rocky Mountain region.

**EASY IDENTIFICATION** Four large photographs plus one illustration are used to visually describe specific plant parts and habitats. Identification tips on the left side of each spread highlight unique features ensuring positive identification.

**COLOR CODING** The plants are arranged by plant type (evergreens, deciduous trees, shrubs then wildflowers) and the wildflowers are organized by color. While this does not represent standard scientific practice, it allows easy navigation.

**SYMBOLS** Symbols are used to describe where to find each plant. First, use the life zone symbols to determine which elevations the plant is most commonly found. Next, use the sun and water symbols to key in on *microhabitats*, areas within the life zone which have specific sun and water conditions where the plant grows. For example, a plant in the montane forest requiring full sun grows in open meadows, while a plant requiring partial sun most likely grows within a forest. A plant requiring lots of water grows in bogs or along stream banks while a plant requiring little water grows on sun-baked hillsides. The life zone and microhabitat symbols work together to identify where each plant grows best.

**NAMES** Common names are used at the top of each plant page. People often use different names for the same plant, especially visitors from other regions of the country, so scientific names are provided to ensure a common understanding. Equally important are the meanings behind the names which are described where historical interest allows.

**PLANT FAMILIES AND RELATIVES** Scientists arrange all living things within families which have common features. For example, all dogs, wild and domestic, are organized within the canine family because they all have four legs, canine teeth and a muzzle. Plant families also have common features. This book lists related plants, but does not describe the features of the plant family because the terminology and specifics become too complicated for casual observers.

*family field guide*

# Contents

# Symbols

The following symbols describe several plant characteristics. Look at the symbols, then read the explanations below to understand their meanings.

## WHERE Describes the life zones and elevations where the plant grows

### LOWLAND SHRUB AND FOREST LIFE ZONE

The hottest and driest ecosystem in the Rocky Mountains, the lowland shrub and forest life zone is located between 6,000 and 8,000 feet above sea level or up to 9,000 feet on sunny, south-facing slopes. Plants here are able to survive hot temperatures and dry conditions. The growing season is from April to October.

### MONTANE LIFE ZONE

This life zone occurs from 8,000-10,000 feet above sea level and has warm summer days and cool nights; it never gets really hot. Snow begins falling in mid-September and melts by May, so the growing season is from late May until September.

### SUBALPINE LIFE ZONE

Cold and shady, the subalpine life zone occurs from 10,000 feet above sea level to treeline (12,500 feet). The forests are snow-covered into June and the meadows are boggy in early summer. The growing season is from June through September.

### ALPINE TUNDRA

Cold and windy, the alpine tundra life zone occurs only above treeline between 12,500-14,433 feet above sea level. Plants here are adapted to high winds, dry soils and a growing season which lasts only from early July through September.

### RIPARIAN ECOSYSTEM

Riparian ecosystems are not classified as a life zone because they occur on the land next to creeks, lakes, rivers and wetlands, rather than at a specific elevation range. They extend from the alpine tundra life zone down to the lowland shrub and forest life zone following the streams and creeks all the while. Plants here like water. The growing season depends on the elevation.

family field guide

# WATER  Describes how much water the plant needs to grow

**LOTS OF WATER**
Needs lots of water; grows near streams, wetlands or seasonal bogs.

**MODERATE WATER**
Gets enough water from melting snow and rain; likes moist soil.

**DRY**
Does not need very much water; likes dry, sunny hillsides or meadows.

# SUN  Describes how much sun the plant needs to grow

**LOTS OF SUN**
Requires bright sun most of the day; grows in open meadows.

**PARTIAL SUN**
Needs part sun and part shade; grows within the shade of the forest.

**SHADE LOVING**
Grows best with shade and a little sun.

# SPECIAL QUALITIES  Describes special qualities of the plant

**EDIBLE**
Parts of this plant can be eaten by people.

**MEDICINAL**
Parts of this plant are commonly used for medicinal purposes.

**GARDEN VARIETIES**
Types of this plant can be purchased in stores and planted in gardens.

**POISONOUS**
Do not eat this plant; it is poisonous to humans or to wildlife.

*family field guide*

# Common Features

## PHOTOSYNTHESIS

Plants do not move around to find food; instead, they make their own. Within green leaves are cells called *chloroplasts* which organize ingredients and make food. The ingredients are sunlight, water and carbon dioxide and the foods they make are sugars or *carbohydrates*. The sugar is used as energy, just as we use food, so that the plant can grow, make seeds and store extra energy to use later. When animals eat plants, they are eating the stored energy in seeds, leaves or fruits. Energy moves from the sun, to plants then to animals in the food chain, all thanks to the photosynthesis. Oxygen is also produced, and is not used by the plant; It is released into the air which, of course, is very helpful to animals which breath this byproduct.

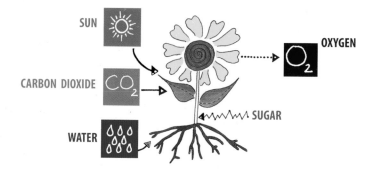

## POLLINATION

The purpose of flowers is not to decorate mountainsides, but to make babies! Babies are made when boy cells touch girl cells. Boy cells in plants are called *pollen* and girl cells are called *eggs*. A plant's goal is to move pollen into the *ovary,* where eggs are stored. Plants cannot move, so they use animals or wind to move the pollen. Most flowers smell very strong, have bright colors or produce a sugary syrup called nectar that attracts insects and birds to land on the flower, touch the pollen and carry it to the eggs of another flower. In the case of evergreen trees, pollen is produced by male cones, blows in the wind and is carried to female cones on other trees. Some plants grow both girl cells and boy cells on the same plant (Alder, Birch and most wildflowers), while other plants (Cottonwoods, Aspen and some wildflowers) have girl cells and boy cells growing on different plants.

## FLOWER PARTS

Use the drawing to identify the main parts of each flower. Some flowers have all of the parts, some do not; some have one of each, while others have many of each part.

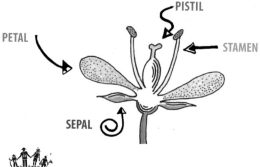

*family field guide*

# Life Zone Indicators

## INDICATOR SPECIES

Indicator species are plants which are representative of a certain habitat or other condition. The plants in this diagram grow almost entirely within a certain life zone or within the riparian ecosystem. Identifying the plants listed below allows you to know where you are on the mountain and which other plants may be growing there.

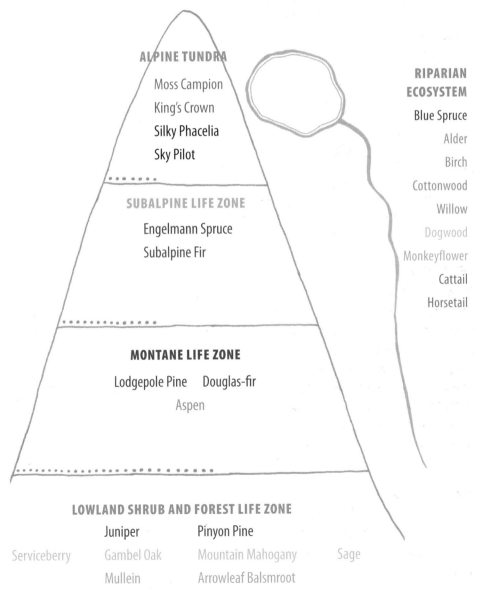

**ALPINE TUNDRA**

Moss Campion

King's Crown

Silky Phacelia

Sky Pilot

**RIPARIAN ECOSYSTEM**

Blue Spruce

Alder

Birch

Cottonwood

Willow

Dogwood

Monkeyflower

Cattail

Horsetail

**SUBALPINE LIFE ZONE**

Engelmann Spruce

Subalpine Fir

**MONTANE LIFE ZONE**

Lodgepole Pine    Douglas-fir

Aspen

**LOWLAND SHRUB AND FOREST LIFE ZONE**

Juniper        Pinyon Pine

Serviceberry    Gambel Oak    Mountain Mahogany    Sage

Mullein    Arrowleaf Balsmroot

family field guide

# Blue Spruce

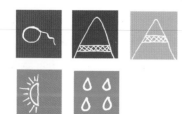

## Pine Family

*Picea pungens*

**ROCKY MOUNTAIN RELATIVES**
Engelmann Spruce

**EASY IDENTIFICATION**
Grow along river banks; single needles roll between fingers; cones longer than a middle finger

**Cones** New female cone in spring (top) matures by summer (bottom); fingernail-sized male cones make pollen (center).

**STATE TREE** Colorado school children voted the Blue Spruce as Colorado's state tree on Arbor Day in 1892. Forty-seven years later, in 1939, Colorado government officials agreed and the Colorado Blue Spruce became the official state tree. It is currently the inspiration for the Colorado State Forest logo.

**THE NATION'S BIGGEST** Colorado recorded the largest Blue Spruce in the nation for over fifty years until a larger one was discovered in Utah in 2001. If you find a big Blue Spruce, get out your tape measure and see if the tree measures more than 190 inches (15 feet 10 inches) around!

**NEEDLE IDENTIFICATION** Remember the saying, "square, spiky, spruce." Spruce needles roll easily between your fingers because they are square in cross-section and they are stiff enough to poke your skin. The Latin name *pungens* means "sharp."

**HOW BABIES ARE BORN** Brush up against any evergreen tree in spring and notice the orange or yellow dust that blows in the air. This dust is *pollen* which is produced in fingernail-sized male cones. The pollen blows in the wind, and when it lands in the scales of a female cone, the egg inside the cone is *fertilized*, meaning that it can grow into a seed. When that seed falls to the ground, it can grow into a mature tree if given the right amount of sun and water and if it is not eaten by animals.

*family field guide*

## SQUIRREL FOOD

Pine Squirrels collect spruce cones, pull the scales apart and eat the seeds inside. Piles of empty scales collect beneath *feeding trees*.

## COLORADO'S BIGGEST

153 feet tall

153 inches around

## CONE

Blue Spruce cones look just like Engelmann Spruce cones, but are larger.

## NEEDLES

Needles are simply a unique type of leaf. By keeping green leaves all year long, evergreens begin photosynthesizing as soon as temperatures are warm enough for water to move through the plant.

## GARDEN PLANT

Blue Spruce is one of the most commonly used evergreens in landscaping because of the blue-tinted needles.

**Color** Spruce needles have a bluer color than pines and firs.

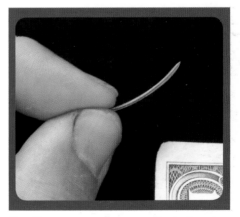

**Needles** Spruce needles grow individually and roll easily between your fingers.

*family field guide*

# Douglas-fir

## Pine Family

*Pseudotsuga menziesii*

**ROCKY MOUNTAIN RELATIVES**
None

**EASY IDENTIFICATION**
Unique cone; flat needles; grow mostly in montane forests

**Female Cone** Look for the "tail" and "hind legs" sticking out between the scales.

**DOUGLAS THE MOUSE** Once upon a time there was a mouse named Douglas. Douglas was a troublesome little mouse and would sneak out at night and steal the seeds from evergreen cones simply to tease the squirrels. His mother worried that night-time predators, especially owls or coyotes, would catch him, so she went to a wise man of the forest and asked for advice. "Warn him that from now on, a curse will be placed on the trees," said the old wise man. "At midnight each evening, the cones of these trees will snap shut, closing off the seeds to any nighttime thieves." Douglas' mother went home and delivered the message. Douglas went out again that night thinking the story was his mother's way of tricking him into staying home. That night, just as Douglas was tipping his head into a cone to steal the seeds, the cone snapped shut trapping Douglas inside. Sadly, he has been trapped ever since that night. To this day, when looking at a Douglas-fir cone, notice Douglas' tail and hind legs sticking out from the cone. This is the easiest way to identify the Douglas-fir tree.

**UNRELATED** Douglas-fir is its own genus of trees and is not related to other firs. There are three species of Douglas-fir trees in the world. Douglas-firs and true Firs both have flat, friendly needles, but Douglas-fir cones drop to the ground while the cones of true Fir trees do not.

*family field guide*

## NEEDLES

Remember the saying, "flat, friendly, fir." Douglas-fir needles grow in singles and do not roll between your fingers because they are flat in cross-section. Also, they are very flexible and do not poke the skin when touched.

## CHRISTMAS TREE

Because the needles are flexible and fragrant, Douglas-fir trees create a nice smell and don't poke anxious children as they dive under the tree on Christmas morning. Fir trees and Douglas-fir trees have long been favorite holiday decorations.

**Male Cone** Small male cones (left) grow in clusters. Their pollen blows into the large female cones.

**Needles** The needles do not roll between your fingers because they are flat.

# Engelmann Spruce

## Pine Family

*Picea engelmannii*

**ROCKY MOUNTAIN RELATIVES**
Blue Spruce

**EASY IDENTIFICATION**
Grow in the highest forests; single needles roll easily between fingers; cones clustered in treetops hang downward

**Female Cone** Female cones look similar to those of Blue Spruce, but are smaller.

**HAPPY TOGETHER** Engelmann Spruce trees grow alongside Subalpine Fir trees in the highest, coldest, snowiest forests of the Rocky Mountains. Spruce-fir forests receive up to 15 feet of snow each winter. Their pyramid-shape allows the branches to droop under the weight of new snow so that snow falls off the branches without breaking them. Aspen branches aren't arranged this way, so their branches often break under the weight of heavy snow.

**GIRLS ON TOP** Like all evergreen trees, Engelmann Spruce trees have male and female cones, which are strategically arranged on the tree. Male cones, located at the bottom of the tree, are the size of a fingernail and produce pollen which blows in the air. Female cones are the larger woody cones which are clustered at the top of the tree. When the wind blows, the pollen is likely going to pollinate a neighboring tree, not itself, because wind rarely blows straight up.

**AN UNUSUAL SMELL** When walking through spruce-fir forests, it is common to smell a salty stink in the air and to notice dense clusters of needles on the trees. These clusters often look like bird or squirrel nests and are caused by a fungus called Witch's Broom. The fungus grows on the tree and causes rapid needle growth in an effort to outgrow the fungus. This fungus usually does not harm the tree and wildlife use these needle clusters for nesting or as resting pads.

*family field guide*

## WITCH'S BROOM

These needle clusters are the result of a harmless fungus called Witch's Broom.

## LONG-LIVED

If left uncut, these trees live 250-450 years old.

## SQUIRREL FOOD

In fall, when Pine Squirrels are preparing for winter, they snip off the cones and bury them around the base of the tree as a winter food supply.

## SLOW-GROWING

Engelmann Spruce trees grow very slowly because they live in subalpine forests where the growing season is short. A tree with a trunk the size of an adult's waist may be 100 years old!

## COLORADO'S BIGGEST

135 feet tall

146 inches around

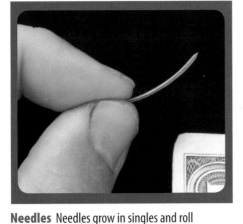

**Needles** Needles grow in singles and roll easily between the fingers.

**Habitat** Engelmann Spruce grow in the highest forests alongside Subalpine Fir.

# Juniper
## (Rocky Mountain Juniper)

## Cypress Family

### Juniperus scopulorum

**ROCKY MOUNTAIN RELATIVES**
Common Juniper

**EASY IDENTIFICATION**
Scaly needles; shaggy bark; blue berries; grow on hot, dry hillsides alongside Pinyon Pine

**Needles and Cones** Scaly needles and bluish cones, which look like berries, are unique.

**GOOD BURNING, BAD BUILDING** Juniper is used for firewood because it burns slow and hot and it smells good. It is used for making fence posts because it is sturdy and does not rot, but because its trunk is twisted and warped it is rarely used for other kinds of construction.

**BERRIES OR CONES?** The bluish "berries" on Junipers are actually female cones. These cones are made up of 3-8 scales which are laid out like the bones of a baby's skull to form a circle. In the beginning, there are spaces between the scales so that pollen can blow between the cracks and land in the center of the cone where the seed will grow. Once the pollen gets inside and the seed begins to grow, the scales grow together like the bones of a skull. As the seed is growing, the cone is green for one year, then turns blue its second year before it is either eaten or falls off the tree.

**A GOOD RELATIONSHIP** Birds and trees often work together to survive. Many birds eat Juniper "berries." They digest the blue fruit, while the seed inside remains whole. As the bird flies to another perch, it poops out the seed which lands in a new place, far from the parent! The tree provides food for the bird and the bird plants the seed. This relationship, where both the bird and the plant benefit, is called a *mutualistic* relationship.

*family field guide*

## SLOW-GROWING AND LONG-LASTING

Juniper trees live in an environment that is very hot and dry. Other evergreen trees become weak and are easily attacked by insects or disease in these conditions, but Juniper trees thrive here. Because of the dryness, Junipers grow very slowly, but large trees in Colorado may be 200-300 years old. The oldest ever recorded was nearly 1,900 years old!

## COLORADO'S BIGGEST

43 feet tall

115 inches around

## WORLDWIDE RELATIVES

There are 27 different Juniper species in the world.

## SWEET SMELLING

When cut or burned, Juniper smells like the shavings in a hamster cage. Those shavings come from Cedar trees and are used to cover up the smell of the hamster. Juniper and Cedar are both in the Cypress family and have many similar characteristics.

**Habitat** Juniper trees grow in hot, dry conditions and are among the hardiest of all evergreens.

**Bark** Juniper bark is "shaggy" and distinct from other evergreen trees.

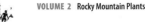

# Lodgepole Pine

# Pine Family

*Pinus contorta*

**ROCKY MOUNTAIN RELATIVES**
Pinyon, Bristlecone and Ponderosa Pines

**EASY IDENTIFICATION**
Paired needles; tight cones; grow on sunny, moist hillsides

**Cone** *Serotinous cones* explode when heated by forest fires.

**BUILT FOR FIRE** Lodgepole Pines grow on sunny hillsides where forest fires are common. To survive fires, they have two types of cones: one for normal seed production and a second, called a *serotinous cone*, which is designed to burst open when heated to over 120 degrees Fahrenheit. If a fire strikes a Lodgepole Pine forest, the temperature rises and the serotinous cones explode, shooting millions of seeds into the air to land in the newly fertile soil. The living trees may die, but the seeds are sown for a new forest to replace the burned one.

**PIONEERS** Plants that grow quickly following a fire, avalanche or other disturbance are called *pioneer species*. Lodgepole Pines are the first trees to grow after a fire has torched a montane forest. They grow very fast in full sunlight, and are very important for shading and nourishing the soil so that slower growing plants can grow in their shade.

**DUFF** Needles regularly dry out, fall off their branches and land on the ground creating a layer of dry needles on the forest floor. This layer of dried needles is called *duff*. Pine needles are *acidic*, so as they collect on the ground and then decay the soil becomes acidic, too. The plant life beneath pine forests is less diverse than other forest types because most plants do not like acidic soil. However, several plant species grow very commonly in the duff because they prefer acidic soil.

*family field guide*

## HOT AND WET

Lodgepole Pines need a lot of sunlight to grow. They can endure very hot temperatures, but unlike Juniper and Pinyon Pine, Lodgepole Pines need a moderate amount of water.

## LONG, STRAIGHT AND FAST

Lodgepole Pines get their name from their long, straight trunks. These "poles" have long been used for building houses and other shelters. Today, Lodgepole Pines are still one of the most commonly cut tree species because of their long, straight trunks and because they grow so fast.

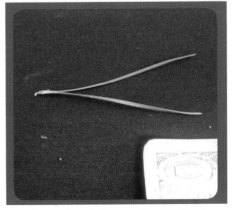

## COLORADO'S BIGGEST

99 feet tall

95 inches around

**Habitat** Lodgepole Pine forests are sunny and produce tall straight trees.

**Needles** Lodgepole Pine needles grow in pairs often the length of a pinky finger.

# Pinyon Pine

## Pine Family

*Pinus edulis*

**ROCKY MOUNTAIN RELATIVES**
Lodgepole, Bristlecone and Ponderosa Pines

**EASY IDENTIFICATION**
Needles in pairs; grow on hot dry hillsides along with Juniper

**Cones** Female cones are green in spring, turn woody in summer, then open in fall.

**PINYON FARMERS** Pinyon Jays specialize in collecting Pinyon seeds, or pine nuts, which grow inside the cones. They collect hundreds of nuts in fall when the cones open, and bury them for later. While all Jays are known for their good memories, sometimes they forget their storage sites. In this way, Pinyon Pine seeds are neatly planted by very busy "farmers."

**GOOD FOOD** Pine nuts have over 3,000 calories per pound and are also very high in protein which makes people strong. By comparison, one pound of Quarter Pounders contains 2,040 calories. Pine nuts have long been an important food for people and animals. Author Edwin Waye Teale wrote, "every autumn, from times uncounted, the calendar of the Ute Indians contained as one of the great, gala events of the years the annual expedition to the mountains for the nuts of the pinyon pine... the pine nuts or Indian nuts of the dry areas of the west played an important part in shaping the lives of the Indians there. Abundant (and) nourishing,...they formed the staple food of winter." The Anasazi Indians also depended on the nuts. Today, pinyon pine nuts are enjoyed in Pesto dishes and salads. Pinyon Jays, Clark's Nutcrackers, black bear, mule deer, turkeys, mice, porcupines and chipmunks all depend on pine nuts. It is legal to collect these nuts, but be sure to consider their importance to wildlife first!

*family field guide*

## TOO SCRAWNY

Pinyon Pine trees are not used for paper or building supplies because they do not grow tall or straight.

## LONG-LIVED, SLOW-GROWING

Pinyon Pines are one of the most drought resistant of all pine trees. They may grow only one inch in diameter every decade, but dominant trees in a stand are likely 400 years old; 800-1,000 year old Pinyon Pines have been recorded.

## STATE TREE

Pinyon Pine is New Mexico's state tree.

## NAME

The Latin name *edulis* means "edible," referring to the tasty pine nut.

## COLORADO'S BIGGEST

48 feet tall

150 inches around

**Habitat** Pinyon Pine grow in the hottest, driest conditions alongside Juniper and Sage.

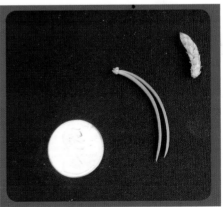

**Needles** Pinyon needles form in pairs and are shorter than an adult's thumb. Male cones (right) form pollen.

*family field guide*

# Ponderosa Pine

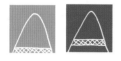

## Pine Family

*Pinus ponderosa*

**ROCKY MOUNTAIN RELATIVES**
Lodgepole, Bristlecone and Pinyon Pines

**EASY IDENTIFICATION**
Needles grow in threes and are longer than a hand-length

**Cones** These are the biggest cones of any Colorado pine. They look like small pineapples before they turn woody and open.

**SUIT OF ARMOR** Forest fires kill trees by burning the buds, roots and *cambium* (a layer below the bark where new growth occurs). Ponderosa Pines have long needles to protect the buds, bark as thick as an index finger to protect the cambium, and their roots extend 4-6 feet below the soil where they are safe from fire. Old Ponderosa Pines have thicker bark and deeper roots and are better protected than young trees.

**BIG ROOTS** Ponderosa Pines are among the tallest trees in Colorado. To support such a huge body, these pines need to have huge roots. Their roots commonly extend 75 feet out from the center, or as far as half a football field from tip-to-tip!

**FINE FOODS** Ponderosa Pine seeds are a favorite food of squirrels, chipmunks and birds, but are not commonly eaten by people. However, Meriwhether Lewis noted in 1805, "I observed many pine trees which appear to have been cut down...in order to collect the seed of the Longleafed Pine which in those moments of distress also furnishes an article of food."

**ANCIENT FIREWORKS** When the Nez Perce Indians were preparing to leave the Lewis and Clark expedition, they wanted to provide an evening of entertainment. They set fire to the trees (mostly Ponderosa Pines) creating a natural fireworks display that quickly ended and caused little damage.

*family field guide*

## DUFF

Dead needles fall to the ground and form a thick layer of decaying material called *duff*. Pine duff is *acidic*, so any plants growing in pine forests must grow well in acidic soil.

## PREDATORS

Rabbits, hares and pocket gophers eat many Ponderosa seedlings while squirrels and porcupines deform the young stems by nibbling on the nutritious shoots.

## OLD GIANTS

Big Ponderosa Pines are commonly 300-600 years old.

## COLORADO'S BIGGEST

160 feet tall

180 inches around

**Bark** Ponderosa Pine bark is thick to protect against fire damage.

**Needles** Ponderosa needles grow in groups of three and are as long as an open hand.

# Subalpine Fir

## Pine Family

*Abies bifolia*

**ROCKY MOUNTAIN RELATIVES**
None

**EASY IDENTIFICATION**
Grow in subalpine life zone; flat needles; cones are difficult to see; silver bark

**Habitat** Subalpine Fir grows alongside Engelmann Spruce in the subalpine life zone.

**HIDDEN CONES** Subalpine Fir cones are purple and stand straight up. They are very difficult to see. Unlike other evergreens in the region, fir trees do not drop their cones. Instead, the cones dry out after the seeds are produced and the scales fall off one at a time leaving only a center spike. Occasionally birds will snip off a few cones which may drop to the forest floor, but within days the cones dry up and fall apart. Unlike other trees which can be identified by their cones, Subalpine Firs are best identified by the "absence" of cones.

**KEEPERS OF WATER** Subalpine Firs live in the highest forests alongside Engelmann Spruce trees. These spruce-fir forests are the coolest and shadiest forests of the Rocky Mountains. Little sunlight reaches the forest floor and the temperature is often five degrees cooler than in neighboring meadows. Snow often remains beneath Subalpine Firs into early June. The shade provided by spruce-fir forests acts like a dam in a reservoir: the snow melts slowly releasing water a bit at a time so that it can seep into the soil and the groundwater table. The water that flows down the steep mountainsides does so slowly without eroding the soil, thanks, in part, to the cool shade of the spruce-fir forests.

**THIN BARK** Subalpine Fir bark is very thin and does not protect from fires. Because they grow where the ground remains moist, fires are very uncommon in spruce-fir forests.

*family field guide*

## STRANGE CONES

While most evergreen cones hang down from their branches, Subalpine Fir cones stand straight up in the air like waxy candles.

## SMALL FIR

There are 14 different Fir species in the world. Subalpine Fir is the smallest of them all.

## WINTER ADAPTATION

When snow accumulates around the bottom branches of a tree, some of the branches get matted against the ground and become imbedded in the soil. When this happens, the imbedded branch may grow roots and become a new tree growing next to the parent. This type of new growth is called *vegetative reproduction* because a new tree is produced without requiring a seed.

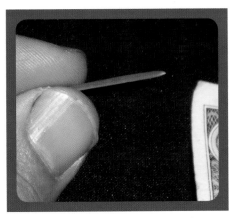

photo by National Park Service

**Needles** The needles grow in singles and do not roll between your fingers.

**Cone** Fir cones do not drop off the tree. If the seeds are not eaten, the cone dries up and falls apart.

# Alder
## (Mountain Alder)

# Birch Family

## Alnus incana

**ROCKY MOUNTAIN RELATIVES**
River Birch

**EASY IDENTIFICATION**
Grow along river banks; fingernail-sized "cones"

**Leaf** Unique leaves with *toothed* edges and parallel veins.

**CATKINS** *Catkin* is a fancy word that describes a cluster of tiny flowers in deciduous trees. These flowers are not colorful or nice-smelling, but they are important because the boy catkins carry pollen and the girl catkins carry eggs. Female Alder catkins are round, fingernail-sized "cones" and male catkins look like droopy, scaly worms. Wind blows the pollen from the male catkin to the female catkin and a new seed begins to grow.

**KEEPER OF THE SOIL** Mountain Alder only grows on the edges of riverbanks and in wetlands where its roots stay wet. In return, the roots hold the soil so that it doesn't erode into the river. Alder roots also contain a bacteria which collects nitrogen from the air, mixes it with oxygen and makes the nitrogen useful for plants. Without these bacteria, nitrogen moves through the soil, but plants are not able to use it. All plants need nitrogen (most fertilizers contain a lot of it), so the presence of Alder roots on a river bank helps all plants to thrive.

**VEGETATIVE GROWTH** Besides growing from seeds, Mountain Alder can send roots out from the parent plant and new trees will poke through the soil directly from these parent roots. By growing from these roots, Alder communities are often very dense and tangled and hard to walk through. They provide excellent shelter for birds and small mammals.

*family field guide*

## FALL COLORS

Alder leaves turn red or brown in fall, but are not very bright.

## WORLDWIDE RELATIVES

There are 14 different Alder species in the world, many of which are large deciduous trees.

## A SHRUB OR A TREE?

Mountain Alder appears more like a shrub than a tree, but can grow upwards of 20 feet tall. Rather than one primary trunk, it grows many thin trunks which create a shrubby thicket of a plant.

## COLORADO'S BIGGEST

48 feet tall
39 inches around

**Cone** Female catkins at left and male catkins at right. These are the reproductive parts of Alder.

**Bark** Alder bark is smooth; it is very different from Birch bark which is bumpy.

*family field guide*

# Aspen
## (Quaking Aspen)

## Willow Family

### Populus tremuloides

**ROCKY MOUNTAIN RELATIVES**
Willows, Cottonwoods

**EASY IDENTIFICATION**
Light colored bark; branches toward the treetop; "eyes" on the bark; heart-shaped leaves

**Leaves** Leaves are nearly heart-shaped with bright veins.

**CLONES** Aspen trees produce seeds, but they usually reproduce from their roots. As roots extend out from the parent tree, *root suckers* shoot up above ground and new trees grow. Sometimes thousands of trees growing side-by-side in one grove are all formed from the same root, all respond to fall color changes at the same time, all begin growing leaves at the same time in spring and all are genetically the same. Plants that are identical are called *clones*.

**SUN LOVER** Aspen trees allow sunshine to reach the ground so that young saplings can grow. The leaves of adult plants dangle in the breeze allowing sunlight to pass through and the lower branches fall off so that they don't shade the forest floor.

**SUCCESSION** Aspen trees are the first trees to grow into avalanche clearings. They love sunshine, grow very fast, and produce new trees quickly from *root suckers* allowing them to colonize easily in newly formed meadows. As they grow taller, they shade the ground slightly, encouraging other plants to grow. Evergreen seeds may land in a shady spot beneath a bush and begin to germinate. As the evergreen grows, it shades the ground which encourages more evergreens to grow. As the evergreens spread, they shade out the sun-loving plants and, within a hundred years or so, the sunny, old grove is a dark, shady forest again.

*family field guide*

## AGING

Aspen tree trunks range in color from bright white to tan and are very smooth, but grow rougher with age. Aspen trees are fast growing and short-lived, rarely surviving more than 100 years.

## FALL COLORS

## EYES

The "eyes" on aspen trunks are scars from old branches which have fallen off. As a tree grows taller, the lower branches fall off the tree allowing more sunlight to reach the forest floor.

## LEAVES

Aspen leaves dangle in the wind allowing sunlight to reach the forest floor.

## WILDLIFE

Black bear, deer, beaver, porcupine, elk, moose, small mammals such as mice, voles, shrews, chipmunks, and rabbits and many birds live and feed in fertile aspen forests.

## SEEDS

Catkins form in spring.

**Summer Aspen grove**

**Fall Aspen grove**

**Winter Aspen grove**

# Birch
## (Water Birch, River Birch)

# Birch Family

*Betula occidentalis*

**ROCKY MOUNTAIN RELATIVES**
Mountain Alder

**EASY IDENTIFICATION**
Toothed leaves; grow along river banks

**Leaf** River Birch leaves are heart-shaped with *toothed* edges and are shiny on top.

**CATKINS** Like Mountain Alder, River Birch has male and female *catkins*. Male catkins produce pollen, are long, brown and droop downward. Female catkins produce eggs, are shorter and stand straight up. These catkins, or flower clusters, are high in nutrients and are a favorite food for birds. People sometimes collect them to add a little flavor to their garden salad.

**LENTICELS** Birch bark is covered in small holes called *lenticels*. These tiny holes allow oxygen and other gases to move in and out of the tree. Plants need nitrogen, carbon dioxide, oxygen and other gases to survive. There is little space for these gases in the soil along riverbanks because water fills the spaces in the soil. Lenticels act like thousands of nostrils allowing the tree to absorb gases from the air because they are not availale to the roots.

**MANY USES** Though people use River Birch for little more than an occasional fence post (the wood is very strong), it is a very important species along the river bank: its fruit is ripe in spring, just as migratory birds are arriving in the mountains, beaver clip the branches to build dams and lodges, their dense growth helps prevent soil erosion along the stream banks and sapsuckers love the sweet sap, then other birds eat the insects that get stuck. Though it is not an outstanding shrub, Water Birch is very important to the riparian community.

*family field guide*

## FALL COLORS

Birch leaves turn yellow and red in fall mixing into the yellow leaves of Willow and Cottonwood.

## RIPARIAN COMMUNITY

River Birch grows alongside Willow, Alder and Dogwood creating a dense tangle of branches which provides excellent cover for small mammals and protected nesting for birds.

## COLORADO'S BIGGEST

56 feet tall

68 inches around

**Bark** Holes in the bark called *lenticels* allow gases to move in and out of the tree.

**Catkin** Male catkins (above) are brown and droopy. Female catkins stand straight up.

# Cottonwood
## (Narrowleaf Cottonwood)

## Willow Family

### Populus Angustifolia

**ROCKY MOUNTAIN RELATIVES**
Aspen, Willows

**EASY IDENTIFICATION**
Thick bark; long, narrow leaves; grow along river banks

**Leaf** Similar in shape to other willows, Cottonwood leaves are long and skinny.

**RIVER GIANTS** Narrowleaf Cottonwood is the most common native Cottonwood tree in Colorado. It is the largest deciduous tree in river valleys above 6,000 feet and provides important nesting and perching for bald eagles, great blue herons, kingfishers (perching only) and other river-dependent birds.

**STICKY BUDS** In early spring, buds form on the branches which will turn into leaves. Cottonwood buds are yellow and sticky and they fill the air with a sweet springtime scent. If your family parks a car beneath a Cottonwood tree, beware of these sticky buds which cause quite a mess when they fall from the tree.

**PATHWAY OF GREEN** In early spring, like a line of toppling dominoes, Cottonwoods in lower elevations form leaves and this budding process gradually continues to higher elevations. The green of the Cottonwoods is a sign that winter has passed and warmer days are coming.

**SEEDS** The name "Cottonwood" comes from the seeds which are clustered on a white fluff that blows through the air in June and July. Unlike Alder and Birch which have boy parts and girl parts on the same tree, Cottonwoods have male trees and female trees. Only the girl trees form the cottony seeds, which need to land in wet soil with full sunlight within a few days. If the seeds don't *germinate* (start growing) within a week, the seeds die.

*family field guide*

## HUMAN USES

Cottonwood rots easily and warps when it is cut, so it is not commonly used for building.

## FAST-GROWING, SHORT-LIVED

These trees grow very fast, but rarely live more than 150 years.

## COLORADO'S BIGGEST
116 feet tall
164 inches around

## ROOTS

Cottonwood roots grow very fast and cover a huge area. These roots help hold the soil in the river bed, but can be a hassle near buildings and sewage drains where they grow into foundations and pipes.

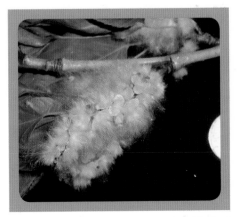

**Bark** Bark is smooth on young plants and grows rougher as the tree gets older.

**Seed** Cottonwood seeds grow as *catkins* which grow only on female trees.

# Chokecherry

## Rose Family

*Prunus virginiana*

**ROCKY MOUNTAIN RELATIVES**
Strawberry, Rose, Raspberry, Serviceberry, Mountain Mahogany and more

**EASY IDENTIFICATION**
Unique flower clusters; red berries turn dark purple when ripe; leaves rounded and finely-*toothed*

**Leaf** The leaves are finely-*toothed*, but look smooth at first glance.

**LONG FLOWER** Chokecherry flowers look like long, fluffy caterpillars. These flowers begin blooming in late May, just as Serviceberry flowers begin to fade.

**CHOKECHERRY JAM** Chokecherries ripen in mid to late August. When ripe, they are very dark in color and grow in long, slender clusters that are the same shape as the flower. They taste very bitter straight from the branch, but with a few heaps of sugar, they are a favorite for making jams and jellies. Following is one chokecherry jam recipe: Remove stems from Chokecherries and wash. Add 1 Cup water to every 4 Cups of fruit. Place over low heat and simmer until fruit is tender, stirring occasionally. Rub pulp through a strainer. Measure this pulp and add an equal amount of sugar. Place over moderate heat and stir until sugar has absorbed. Bring to a rolling boil and cook until the mixture sheets off the spoon. Stir frequently. Pour into sterile jars, leaving $1/4$" empty space at the top. Wipe jar rims, adjust lids and rings. Place sealed jars in boiling water for 10 minutes.

**WILDLIFE LOVE 'EM TOO** Butterflies, moths and bees love the sweet smelling flowers in spring. Bears depend on a good crop of Chokecherries to fatten up in fall before their winter hibernation. Birds eat ripened berries and any leftovers that remain in early winter. Deer and elk browse on Chokecherry twigs in winter.

*family field guide*

## FALL COLORS

Leaves turn pink to red in fall making some of the brightest leaves on the lowland shrub hillside contrasting with yellow and orange Serviceberry and the browns and maroons of Gambel Oak.

## LOWLAND SHRUB COMMUNITY

Chokecherry often grow on hot, dry hillsides along with Gambel Oak, Serviceberry and Mountain Mahogany. Chokecherry shrubs are easy to identify in midsummer because their leaves are bigger and rounder than the leaves of its neighbors.

## BEAR FOOD

Chokecherries and acorns are the two foods that bears depend on most when fattening up for winter.

## LONG AND SKINNY

The flowers and berries both grow in long, skinny bundles.

**Berry** Berries are bright red then darken as they become ripe. They taste very bitter!

**Flower** Chokecherry flowers are easy to identify by their long, slender clusters of tiny flowers.

*family field guide*

# Dogwood
## (Red-Osier Dogwood)

## Dogwood Family

*Cornus stolonifera*

**ROCKY MOUNTAIN RELATIVES**
None

**EASY IDENTIFICATION**
Smooth leaves grow opposite each other; leaves rounder than willows; grow near water; red branches in winter

**Leaf** Dogwood leaves grow opposite each other and the veins run towards the tip.

**WHAT'S THE DIFFERENCE?** Dogwood grow in streamside thickets alongside Willows, Birch and Alder. The tangle of branches make it difficult to tell one plant from the next. Dogwood is the only plant in this shrubby community to grow flowers in spring, white berries in late summer and has rounder, smooth-edged leaves all summer.

**BERRIES** Dogwood berries are white. They are not poisonous, but are not worth eating. Birds, bears, raccoons, chipmunks, squirrels, rabbits and hares, however, love to eat the berries. Best keep them on the branches rather than waste them on your tongue.

**ORNAMENTAL** Many people plant Dogwood in their yards near ponds, irrigation ditches or other wet places. The branches turn bright red in cold winter temperatures. In spring, flowers attract butterflies, moths, bees and birds. In late summer, berries attract small mammals and birds. Red Osier Dogwood is beautiful on its own, and creates a flurry of natural activity in its presence.

**RIPARIAN PLANT** Red Osier Dogwood grows only in *riparian* areas, on the land along the banks of streams, lakes, rivers and in wetlands. Its roots must be wet all the time. Dogwood provides nesting space for birds, branches for beavers and food and cover for migrating mammals.

*family field guide*

## FALL COLORS

Dogwood leaves turn bright red to deep purple in fall.

## WORLDWIDE RELATIVES

There are 27 different Dogwood species, many of which are large trees, very different from this tangly shrub.

## RIPARIAN BEAUTY

Dogwood grows alongside Willow, Birch and Alder in *riparian* areas along streams, rivers and wetlands. These plants form a tangle of branches that provide food and shelter for wildlife and help prevent soil erosion during floods.

**Branches** The name Red Osier refers to the branches which turn deep red in cold weather.

**Berries** White berries form in late summer and are food for wildlife, but not for people.

family field guide

# Elderberry
## (Red Elderberry)

## Honeysuckle Family

### Sambucus racemosa

**ROCKY MOUNTAIN RELATIVES**
Twinberry, Snowberry

**EASY IDENTIFICATION**
Long, pointy leaflets grow opposite each other; white flowers in spring; bright red berries in late summer

**Flower** Clusters of white flowers create formless bunches in spring.

**POISONOUS** The bright red berries are poisonous when eaten raw, but can be cooked and made into wine or jam. The berries are eaten by birds, rabbits, squirrels, foxes and sometimes bears, but if eaten uncooked will cause vomiting and diarrhea in people. Other species of Elderberry produce blue or purple berries which are much sweeter and better for eating.

**SUCCESSION** Elderberry grows best in damp, sunny meadows or aspen groves. They like sun! If an evergreen seed falls in the shade beneath an Elderberry bush, it may grow and eventually cast a shadow on the bush. This new shady area encourages more evergreens to grow and the sunny meadow slowly turns to a shady forest causing the Elderberry bush and other sun-loving plants to die. This process of forest change is called *succession* and occurs slowly, but constantly within ecosystems.

**NAMES** The Latin name *Sambucus* refers to an ancient Greek stringed instrument, the sambuca, which was supposedly made from Elderberry wood. The branches were also boiled, hollowed out and made into flutes and whistles, supporting a less-used common name "tree of music."

**HEIGHT** In dry soils where the plant does not grow fast, Elderberry looks like a scraggly shrub, but in ideal moist conditions it grows very fast and can be as tall as a house.

*family field guide*

## ORNAMENTAL

The bright red berries, unique leaves and the attraction for birds and other wildlife make this a common shrub for landscaping.

## MOUTHFULL

When bears eat elderberries, they eat the entire bunch in one bite leaving a cleanly snipped branch.

## HOLLOW STEMS

Elderberry stems are hollow. They can be cut and holes can be poked in them to make a natural flute.

## BOIL FIRST

Elderberries contain a chemical which causes vomiting. Boiling the berry breaks down the chemical and makes the berries edible.

**Leaves** The thin pointy leaves grow opposite each other.

**Berry** Bundles of bright red berries are edible when cooked, but are poisonous when eaten raw.

family field guide

# Gambel Oak
## (Scrub Oak)

# Oak Family

*Quercus gambelii*

**ROCKY MOUNTAIN RELATIVES**
None

**EASY IDENTIFICATION**
Unique leaf; acorns in fall; grow on hot, dry hillsides

**Leaf** Gambel Oak leaves are easy to idenify with their gently curving *lobed* shape.

**BIG AND SMALL** Gambel Oaks vary in size from dense shrubby thickets to 20-foot tall trees with trunks as thick as an adult's thigh and a leafy canopy that hangs over an adult's head. The dense thickets are created by cloning (one thicket growing from a single root system), from deer and elk grazing (see "clumping" below) and from growing in areas where water quickly evaporates or drains downhill. The taller trees occur in unburned areas and in flat meadows where water is able to settle into the soil.

**FIRE RESISTANT ROOTS** Forest fires burn frequently through Scrub Oak thickets, especially in October and November when dried leaves remain on the branches or collect on the ground. These fires burn quickly through a grove, but do not burn long enough in one area to get too hot. If the roots do not burn, new oak shrubs will grow immediately from the unharmed roots.

**CLUMPING** Dense oak thickets often look like they've been trimmed to one height. Gambel Oak branches are a favorite winter food for deer and elk and a herd can trim an entire hillside in one winter. When the tips of the branches are cut, the next year's growth occurs outward from the stem, rather than growing longer from the tip. The effect is a clump of growth at the top of each branch which creates a very dense thicket too thick to walk through.

*family field guide*

## LAST LEAVES

These are the last of the lowland shrubs to turn green in spring and the last to change colors in fall.

## BEAR FOOD

Acorns are very important food for bears preparing for hibernation. Some years, acorns are very abundant and bears eat as many as they please. If, however, the *catkins* freeze in the spring, very few acorns grow in the fall and bears must seek other foods, often from dumpsters in towns.

## WORLDWIDE RELATIVES

There are 206 different Oak species, many of which grow as tall deciduous trees.

**Fire** Following a fire, new growth occurs quickly from unharmed roots.

**Acorns** Acorns grow in late summer and are an important food for bears and rodents.

*family field guide*

# Mountain Mahogany

## Rose Family

*Cercocarpus montanus*

**ROCKY MOUNTAIN RELATIVES**
Strawberry, Rose, Raspberry, Serviceberry

**EASY IDENTIFICATION**
Small, toothed leaves; feathery seeds in fall; grow on hot, dry hillsides

**Flower** Small yellowish flowers grow in spring, then turn into screwy seeds in fall.

**OVERLOOKED PLANT** Mountain Mahogany grows alongside Serviceberry and Gambel Oak on hot, dry hillsides. It is very easy to miss; it does not produce berries, its leaves are not brightly colored in the fall and its flowers in spring are tiny. Nonetheless, Mountain Mahogany is one of the hardiest and most common plants on these lowland hillsides. A person can chop it with an axe, yet it will continue to grow from the stump. A fire can burn it, but a new plant will grow from the roots. During a long drought, it will shrink in size to conserve energy, but will continue to grow again when conditions are right.

**SCREWY SEEDS** The most unique part of Mountain Mahogany is its seeds, which are small, feathery and spun like a corkscrew. The seeds form in fall, when the leaves are changing colors. When the wind blows, these seeds fly off the branch and spin a good distance away from the parent. Upon landing, this spinning motion allows the seeds to "screw" a few millimeters into the ground where it is more likely to *germinate* (grow).

**WINTER FOOD** Mountain Mahogany is an important winter food source for deer and elk. When grasses are covered, seeds are no longer around, leaves are not growing and there is nothing green to eat, dried Mahogany twigs provide just enough nutrition to keep these big animals alive until spring.

*family field guide*

## FALL COLORS

Leaves turn brown and sometimes yellow, but are not very bright.

## EROSION CONTROL

Snow melts from the lowland shrub hillsides by mid-April and is bone-dry by late June. Water that falls from late summer storms can cause severe erosion on these dry hillsides. Mountain Mahogany and other shrubs are important because their roots hold the soil in place.

## SHELTER

Mountain Mahogany is a very dense shrub that grows in tight thickets that are difficult to walk through. The tangle of branches provides protection for small mammals and safety for ground-nesting birds.

**Leaf** The leaves are asymmetrical; the left side is different from the right.

**Seed** The seed is very unique and looks like a whirling feather.

# Raspberry

## Rose Family

*Rubus idaeus*

**ROCKY MOUNTAIN RELATIVES**
Strawberry, Rose, Serviceberry, Chokecherry and more

**EASY IDENTIFICATION**
Thorny stems; pointy leaves; sunny slopes

**Leaf** Leaflets grow opposite each other and are very pointy.

**FRUIT OF THE VINE** Raspberries are probably the most recognizable fruit in the Rocky Mountains. The fruits look like raspberries from the grocery store, but are about the size of a pinky fingernail instead of a thumbnail. Bears, birds and rodents eat raspberries too, so if you find a patch, take a few, but leave some for the animals. Pick them carefully as the branches are thorny like a rose bush.

**PREGNANT MOMS LOVE 'EM** The leaves are not good to eat, but a lot of pregnant mothers pick the leaves, dry them, boil them in water then drink the tea to help them feel better during pregnancy. Raspberry teas are sold in stores for this reason, but fresh leaves are more effective.

**RASPBERRIES AND ROSES** Some people look for Raspberry patches in summer so they can return in August to collect the fruit. In summer, however, Raspberry plants look very similar to Roses. To quickly identify a raspberry plant, look first for the thorny twigs, then compare the leaves to those of a Rose; rose leaves are rounded and raspberries are pointy. Once you've found a good patch, don't tell anybody about it (except maybe your parents) and return in mid-August with a few containers for collecting. A good Raspberry patch provides enough berries to eat, enough to leave for wildlife and enough to take home, too.

*family field guide*

## TINY FLOWERS

Look carefully for Raspberry flowers in spring. The tiny whitish-green petals are difficult to see unless you look carefully.

## ROSE FAMILY

Plants in the rose family produce favorite foods including apples, plums, pears, peaches and more. However, not all plants in this family make tasty fruits including Mountain Mahogany and Cinquefoil. Though not all plants in this family produce fruit, they all have similar flower parts.

## HOT AND SUNNY

Raspberries grow best in sandy soil with full sunlight. They often grow in open meadows or in small clearings within the forest.

**Flower** The flower is very unique with petals so small they are difficult to see!

**Berry** Bright red berries form in late summer and are delicious trail snacks.

# Rose
## (Wild Rose, Wood Rose)

# Rose Family

*Rosa woodsii*

**ROCKY MOUNTAIN RELATIVES**
Strawberry, Raspberry, Mountain Mahogany, Serviceberry, Cinquefoil and more

**EASY IDENTIFICATION**
Thorny branches; rounded, toothed leaves grow opposite each other; rocky soil

**Leaf** Leaflets grow opposite each other, are *toothed* at the top and a bit rounded.

**SEEDY HIPS** After the Wild Rose flower has dried up, a fruit begins to grow. The berries on rose plants are called Rose Hips. They are very healthy; some reports say there is more Vitamin C in one berry than in an entire orange. However, these fruits are anything but juicy and there are so many seeds inside that you find yourself spitting out the whole fruit. The berries are best put in a pot of boiling water for tasty tea.

**NATIONAL BEAUTY** Wild Rose has long been a favorite flower of many and was in the running for our nation's national floral emblem for decades before President Reagan approved its status in 1986. Following is a letter to the editor in Time magazine from July 15, 1929: "(While reading) the May Nature magazine, I discovered that the subject of a national flower is being brought forward by that magazine and in the poll of votes printed, the wild rose was running far ahead of the columbine. Now, in my estimation, the reason for this popularity of the wild rose, is because of its aggressive assertion of itself. It is thorny and disagreeable to the touch, a thing we do not want in a national flower. If it is picked, it wilts in a few minutes. It comes out a beautiful pink, but before it dies it has faded to a colorless existence. Farmers root it out, as its luxuriant growth soon ruins the fences over which it sprangles. Not one of the phases of its short life is connected with our desires in a national emblem."

*family field guide*

## FALL COLORS

The leaves turn yellow, copper, orange and dark maroon in fall.

## WILDLIFE LIKE THEM

Squirrels, deer, coyotes and bears eat the ripe berries. Birds eat leftover berries in winter. Porcupine and beaver are not afraid of the thorns as Wild Rose leaves are among their favorite foods.

## ROSE FAMILY

This family of plants includes such favorites as apples, pears, plums, peaches, raspberries, strawberries, serviceberries and more!

**Thorns** Enjoy smelling the flowers, but keep some distance from the thorns!

**Berry** Rose hips grow red and plump. You can eat them but they are more seed than fruit!

*family field guide*

# Sage
## (Mountain Sagebrush)

## Sunflower Family

### Artemisia tridentata

**ROCKY MOUNTAIN RELATIVES**
White Sage, Fringed Sagewort, Dwarf Sagewort, Boreal Sagewort, Wild Tarragon

**EASY IDENTIFICATION**
Three-toothed leaf; woody "trunk"; very fragrant; grow in hot, dry flats

**Leaf** Each leaf has three or four *teeth*, thus the Latin name *tri* (three) *dentata* (teeth).

**DOMINANT** Mountain Sagebrush is the dominant species in flat or rolling pastures that are sunny, hot and dry. Juniper and Pinyon Pine often grow on the hillsides surrounding sage flats, Gambel Oak, Mountain Mahogany and Serviceberry often cover the shrub lands surrounding the flats, but Mountain Sagebrush grows on the flats where no larger trees or shrubs can shade the ground. Wildflowers color the spaces between the shrubs in spring.

**ENDANGERED ECOSYSTEM** Sage communities occur on level open areas, the same sort of place that is good for farming, cattle grazing and housing construction. According to a study conducted in 2001, sage communities have so often been changed from their native form (see Grazing at right), that they are one of the most endangered ecosystems in North America.

**WINTER FOOD** Sagebrush is very low in nutrients and contains special oils that prevent it from being digested. Nonetheless, deer and elk will browse on sage leaves in winter when more nturtious foods are not available. The meat of deer or elk that have been feeding on sage in mid-winter or early spring has a sage-like flavor.

**SWEET SMELLING SAGE** Sagebrush is best known for its distinct smell. The smell is activated by rubbing your fingers against the leaves or by walking through a sage flat after a rainstorm.

*family field guide*

## THREE TEETH

The Latin name *Tridentata* refers to the shape of the leaves. Look carefully at each leaf and notice the three teeth (sometimes four) on the tips.

## WORLDWIDE RELATIVES

There are 68 different sagebrush species in the world.

## EVERGREEN

Mountain Sagebrush leaves remain green through winter allowing it to photosynthesize later into the winter and to begin photosynthesizing immediately in the spring.

## GRAZING

Animals do not like to eat sage, but love the grasses and other plants growing between the sage shrubs. Following intensive grazing, sage flats do not appear disturbed at first glance because the sage plants are not affected. However, other plants growing alongside the sage shrubs may suffer irreparable damage allowing non-native weeds and grasses to alter the original plant community.

**Habitat** Sage is the dominant plant in dry sunny flats and rolling hills.

**Seeds** Seed clusters sprout in late summer and remain as dry stalks through winter.

# Serviceberry
## (Saskatoon Serviceberry)

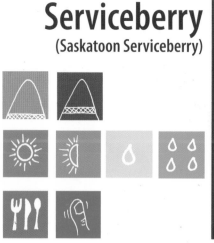

## Rose Family

*Amelanchier alnifolia*

**ROCKY MOUNTAIN RELATIVES**
Strawberry, Rose, Chokecherry, Raspberry

**EASY IDENTIFICATION**
Round, partly-toothed leaves; white flower in spring; purple berry in late summer

**Flower** Serviceberry shrubs flower early each spring, dusting lowland hills in white.

**WINTER LANDSCAPING** Serviceberry (pronounced sarviceberry) can survive very dry conditions. They grow on south-facing slopes where deer and elk graze in winter. In these locations, the shrubs grow in very dense patches rarely taller than six feet high because of intense winter feeding. In areas where deer and elk are not present, the bushes can be 10-15 feet tall.

**EARLY WRITINGS** Meriwether Lewis was the first European to observe and write about this species of Serviceberry. On August 2, 1805 he noted in the language and spelling of the time, "We found a great Courants,...also black goosburies and service buries now ripe and in full perfection, we feasted sumptuously on our wild fruit, particularly the yellow courant and the deep purple service bury which I found to be excellent....The service bury grows on a smaller bush different from ours (in the eastern U.S.) only in colour and the superior excellence of its flavor and size, it is of a deep purple."

**GOOD FOOD** Native Americans in the Rocky Mountain region dried the berries for winter food and added them to cakes and to pemmican made from meat and fat. They used the wood for arrows, the fiber for making rope and the leaves and twigs for medicine. Wildlife also depend on the fruit. In August when the berries are ripe, raccoon, bear and fox scat are often purple with partly digested berries.

*family field guide*

The leaves turn a brilliant yellow, then fade to brown.

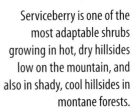

**ADAPTABLE**

Serviceberry is one of the most adaptable shrubs growing in hot, dry hillsides low on the mountain, and also in shady, cool hillsides in montane forests.

**SEASONS**

Berries in August, flowers in May.

**AUTHOR'S CHOICE**

When the berries are ripe in August, they are a favorite native trail snack.

**Berries** The berries are sweet right off the branch!

**Leaf** The leaves are round, smooth at the bottom and *toothed* at the top.

# Willow

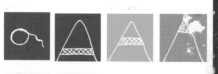

## Willow Family

*Salix*

### ROCKY MOUNTAIN VARIETIES
Alpine, Booth, Sandbar, Planeleaf, Whiplash, Strapleaf Willow and more

### EASY IDENTIFICATION
Grow in wetlands and stream banks; long, thin leaves; "pussy willows" in spring

**Catkins** Willow *catkins* are a sign of spring and are generically called "pussy willows."

**EVERYBODY LIKES WILLOWS** Willows grow in *riparian* areas, the land along stream banks, lake edges and wetlands. More animals depend on riparian areas for food, shelter, water and migration paths than any other ecosystem. Birds use the tangle of branches for nest sites and eat the buds in the spring. Elk, deer and bighorn sheep eat the buds and leaves and beaver eat the sugary layer beneath the bark (*cambium*) and use twigs to build lodges and dams. The branches are dense and tangled providing excellent protection for birds, muskrats and other small mammals.

**SAVE THE STREAM** Willows need to live near water where their roots can stay wet. Like their branches, Willow roots create a tangled web below ground that acts as a barrier that prevents soil erosion. If it were not for the web of Willow roots, stream banks would collapse during spring floods.

**BASKETS AND BEAVERS** Willow branches can be twisted, wrapped and bent without breaking. Skilled weavers including Native Americans and frontier women were able to weave willow baskets tight enough to hold water, grains and other foods they collected. Willow branches were also tied in hoops by trappers; skins were tied to each hoop so they could dry in the sun without warping or shriveling.

*family field guide*

## WORLDWIDE RELATIVES

Thirty-five species of Willow include trees like Cottonwood and Aspen, the other 400 species are shrubby stream bank varieties.

## PUSSY WILLOWS

The soft spring growths often called "pussy willows" are willow flowers, or *catkins*. Male plants have pollen on their catkins, female plants carry eggs in theirs. Insects visit the sweet smelling males, then drop the pollen onto the female catkins where seeds are formed.

## VEGETATIVE REPRODUCTION

Willow branches often snap during storms and floods or from animals that snip them loose. If these branches stick in the mud, they will form roots and grow. This is a form of *vegetative reproduction*.

**Habitat** All varieties of Willows grow along streambanks and wetlands.

**Leaf** Willow leaves vary by species, but all are long and thin and turn yellow in fall.

# Alpine Sunflower
## (Old-Man-of-the-Mountain)

## Sunflower Family

*Tetraneuris grandiflora*

**ROCKY MOUNTAIN RELATIVES**
Daisies, asters, sunflowers, sages, thistles

**EASY IDENTIFICATION**
Short sunflower; grow above treeline

**Flower** This flower is unique to the tundra and always faces east.

**COMPASS FLOWER** This sunflower only grows as tall as a third grader's ankles, but its bright yellow flower looks outstanding in the alpine tundra. Even more outstanding is that the flowers always face east. For this reason, they are often called Compass Flowers.

**PATIENCE** Alpine Sunflower grows a cluster of leaves year after year for decades before it ever produces a flower. Every summer, only three months out of each year, the plant turns sunlight into energy. Some of the energy is used to grow, while the rest is stored for later use. Plants require lots of energy to make pollen, eggs and all of the flower parts. This flower may grow for decades before it has stored enough energy to make a flower. Following a long life of photosynthesizing and energy storage, the plant makes a flower which attracts butterflies, moths and flies which *pollinate* it, then once it is pollinated and forms seeds, it dies.

**WOOLY HAIRS** Notice the tiny hairs growing on the leaves and stem of this sunflower. Though they look too small to be helpful, these hairs help the plant hold onto water when the wind tries to dry out its leaves. Leaves and stems have tiny holes in them called *stomata* which allow oxygen, carbon dioxide and other gases to move in and out of the plant. Each tiny hair protects one of those holes so that when the wind blows, the hole is slightly covered, thus protecting the water inside the leaves.

*family field guide*

## MANY FLOWERS IN ONE

Old-Man-of-the-Mountain is a member of the Sunflower Family which is also called the Composite Family. Composite means a single thing which is made from many smaller things. Each yellow "petal" growing from the center of this and all sunflowers is actually an entire flower. A single Alpine Sunflower plant has many flowers all growing in what appears as a single flower atop the stem!

## PERENNIALS AND ANNUALS

Alpine Sunflower grows back every year for many years before it ever produces a flower. Plants that return each year are called *perennials*. Plants that die after only one year are called *annuals*. In the alpine tundra, the growing season is too short for seeds to germinate, flower and form a seed within a single season, so most alpine plants are perennials.

**Size** This flower is rarely more than six inches tall so it avoids the gusty alpine winds.

**Habitat** Old-Man-Of -The-Mountain grows only above treeline in the alpine tundra.

*family field guide*

# Arnica
## (Heartleaf Arnica)

## Sunflower Family

### Arnica cordifolia

**ROCKY MOUNTAIN RELATIVES**
Clumped Arnica, Subalpine Arnica and Parry's Arnica

**EASY IDENTIFICATION**
Leaves grow in pairs and are toothed

**Flower** Heartleaf Arnica flower is similar to other sunflowers so look carefully at the leaf.

**MEDICINE** Arnica is commonly used as an anti-inflammatory which means that it helps stop swelling. It is dried, ground up and used in creams which are rubbed on the skin to treat bruises, sprains, insect bites and more. Arnica is only used on the skin; it is poisonous to eat. Do not eat this plant!

**WET AND DRY** There are four different species of Arnica growing in Colorado, three of which look like a common yellow sunflower. Clumped Arnica and Subalpine Arnica both grow in wet soils of the Subalpine life zone. Heartleaf Arnica (pictured) grows in dry soils.

**COLONIES** Arnica flowers form feathery seeds that blow on the wind and spread throughout the forest. In some cases, many flowers grow close together in a small colony. These bunches are a single plant growing from underground stems called *rhizomes*. In this way, a single plant can produce many flowers causing more seeds to be planted in the forest.

**SHADE AND SOIL** Heartleaf Arnica grows in open woods where sunlight brightens the forest floor. Lodgepole Pine forests create this partly-shaded environment. However, many plants do not grow well in pine forests because the dried pine needles which fall to the ground make the soil *acidic*. Arnica likes acidic soil which allows it to grow well in these pine forests where other plants cannot.

*family field guide*

## NAMES

The name Arnica comes from a Latin word which means "lamb skin." This description refers to the short, fuzzy hairs on the leaves and stems. The Latin name *cordifolia* means "heart-leaved."

## LONG SEASON

Arnica flowers appear in late May and continue all summer into September.

## DEER FOOD

Arnica is not a main food for most animals, but mule deer eat the flowers. Deer grazing in Lodgepole Pine forests prefer Arnica to most other plants growing in the dried pine needles.

**Leaves** The paired leaves allow easy identification of Heartleaf and Clumped Arnica.

**Seed** After the flower has matured, it turns into a seed desinged to blow in the wind.

# Arrowleaf Balsamroot

## Sunflower Family

*Balsamorhiza sagittata*

**ROCKY MOUNTAIN RELATIVES**
Daisies, asters, sunflowers, sages, thistles

**EASY IDENTIFICATION**
Huge, silvery-green leaves; early spring flowers; grow in lowland shrub and forest

**Leaf** As big as a child's head, the leaves are silvery-green and tough like leather.

**EARLY RISER** Arrowleaf Balsamroot is the first big sunflower to blossom in spring. These bright yellow flowers appear in May and are almost dried up by early June. In their prime, they blanket lowland shrub hillsides in gold. Once the soil dries up, so do the flowers.

**COMPANION PLANTS** The term *companion plants* refers to plants that often grow side-by-side. Arrowleaf Balsamroot grows on the lowland shrub hillsides along with several types of sage, Indian Paintbrush and Scarlet Gilia, to name a few. Juniper and Pinyon Pine often grow on surrounding forested hillsides, but Arrowleaf Balsamroot needs full sunlight and does not grow well in shade.

**ONE TOUGH PLANT** Arrowleaf Balsamroot is a very hardy plant. It can survive in sunny, dry conditions and it grows well in areas that are grazed by cattle and deer. It survives trampling and becomes even more abundant after cattle graze the flower heads.

**FOOD AND MEDICINE** This plant was widely used for medicine and food by native Americans; they peeled and ate the inner part of the young flower stems, ate raw leaves like a salad, seeds were roasted and eaten or ground into flour, roots were baked in a fire for several hours and eaten like a potato. Leaves were used in treating burns and the roots were cut and boiled to make a medicinal tea.

*family field guide*

## MULE'S EAR

A very similar looking plant with equally large leaves called Mule's Ear commonly grows side by side with Arrowleaf Balsamroot. Mule's Ear leaves are ear-shaped and Arrowleaf Balsamroot leaves are arrow-shaped and more leathery.

## BIG ROOT

As its name indicates, this plant grows from a long tap root that digs deep into the soil to anchor the huge leaves and to absorb nutrients and water. The root can grow 5-6 feet deep!

## LONG-LIVED FLOWER

Arrowleaf Balsamroot is a *perennial* which means that it grows back each year. Some plants may live 30-40 years!

**Habitat** Grows on sunny lowland hillsides in early spring along with Mountain Sagebrush.

**Flower** The flower is similar to many sunflowers; use the leaf, season and location for identification.

# Cinquefoil
## (Beauty Cinquefoil)

## Rose Family

*Potentilla gracilis*

### ROCKY MOUNTAIN RELATIVES
Shrubby Cinquefoil, Alpine Cinquefoil, Silver Cinquefoil

### EASY IDENTIFICATION
Leaves are green on the top, silver on bottom and a unique shape

**Flower** These five petals look similar to buttercups. Use the leaf for identification.

**FIVE LEAVES** Cinquefoil means "five leaves" in French. This is good to remember, but does not always describe local Cinquefoil plants as they commonly have 7, 9 or even 15 leaflets, but always an odd number. The bottom side of the leaf is silver in color like aluminum *foil*.

**POTENTILLA** Cinquefoil plants are all part of a genus called Potentilla (pronounced like tortilla) of which there are over 360 different types. Potentillas range from bushy shrubs, which are commonly planted around houses, to wild, leafy flowers like this.

**HYBRIDS** When bees and flies travel from one Potentilla plant to the next, they carry the pollen with them. Occasionally the pollen of one species will land on the eggs of a different species. The new seed will grow a plant that has parts of the mother species and parts of the father species. This process is called *hybridization* and many new plant varieties are created this way. Cinquefoil varieties have so many different hybrids that it is difficult to tell one variety from another.

**POEM** by Ralph Waldo Emerson

For what need I of book or priest,
Or Sibyl from the mummied East,
When every star is Bethlehem star?
I count as many as there are
Cinquefoils or violets in the grass.

*family field guide*

Showy Cinquefoil has several cousins living in other life zones. Silver Cinquefoil lives in drier soils of the lowlands, often in sage communities. Alpine Cinquefoil lives in the tundra. These plants all look very similar. Shrubby Cinquefoil is a shrub with different looking leaves, but a similar flower.

## SUN LOVER

Cinquefoil usually grow in sunny meadows, their leaves and stems tangled among native grasses.

**Leaf** The leaves are a unique shape. They are green on top and silvery-white on the bottom.

**Habitat** These flowers are often tangled among grasses in sunny meadows.

# Dandelion

## Sunflower Family

### Taraxacum officinale

**ROCKY MOUNTAIN RELATIVES**
Daisies, asters, sunflowers, sages, thistles

**EASY IDENTIFICATION**
Round yellow flower in spring and early summer; fluffy seeds; *toothed* leaf; grow in sunny, moist meadows

**Leaf** *Dent-de-lion* means "teeth of the lion" in an ancient language referring to the leaf.

**BEAUTY OR BEAST**  These flowers, originally from Europe, blanket pastures in early June. When pastures are in bloom, they are one of the most striking scenes of early summer. Once the flowers turn to seed and the stems shrivel, they are less brilliant and when they get into landscaped yards, home owners think they are the least brilliant of all flowers.

**WHAT IS A WEED?**  A weed is any plant that is not originally from the area, is unwanted and cannot be controlled. Around homes, Dandelions are considered weeds; they litter the soft green grass with unwanted stems and, even when sprayed, cut and dug out, they continue to grow each season. In natural settings they do not have such a bad reputation because they do not stop native plants from growing. As long as a plant does not prevent native plants from growing, it is not considered a weed in nature.

**IF YOU CAN'T BEAT 'EM...**  While home owners dislike Dandelions, some people love these little plants. Children of course love to pop off the flower heads and sing, "Mamma had a baby and its head popped off." Then there is the unusual child's tale that if you put a Dandelion under a person's chin and it reflects yellow on their skin, then they love butter. There are quite a number of recipes for dandelion jelly, wine, soup and salad. Such rhymes, food and fun prove the saying, "If you can't beat 'em, join 'em."

*family field guide*

## SMART SEEDS

After the golden flowers have dried up, they turn to seeds. Part of the success of Dandelions is the soft parachute-like seed which, when blown by the wind, carry far from the parent plant.

## NON-NATIVE

Dandelions did not grow in the Rocky Mountains originally. They were brought to North America from Europe. Plants that are introduced from other parts of the world are called *non-native* species.

## WEED

Though it is a most hated plant by home owners, Dandelions are not considered an *invasive species* in mountain pastures because they do not prevent native plants from growing.

**Seeds** These seeds are designed to blow in the wind or by the playful breath of children.

**Flowers** The flower is easy to identify as "Mama's baby whose head popped off."

# Glacier Lily
## (Avalanche Lily)

# Lily Family

*Erythronium grandiflorum*

### ROCKY MOUNTAIN RELATIVES
Corn Lily, Mariposa Lily, Wild Onion

### EASY IDENTIFICATION
Unique drooping flower; grow in moist soil

**Flower** Petals fold back allowing pollen to dust the heads of hungry hummingbirds.

*photo by National Park Service*

**FANCY FEAST** Glacier Lilies are tasty. Grizzly bears are known to eat their flowers, stems and roots (bulbs) in the Northern Rockies. According to Meriwether Lewis' journals, the bulbs, leaves, flowers and seed pods were all prepared and eaten by Native Americans. In Colorado, black bears and rodents are known to dig and eat the *bulbs* and the seed pods are a favorite of deer, elk, bighorn sheep and mountain goats.

**FIRST OBSERVATIONS** In 1806 Meriwether Lewis was the first European to collect this plant in present-day Idaho. He misidentified it as Dogtooth Violet, a similar looking plant common in the eastern states.

**EARLY BLOOMER** Glacier Lilies bloom early in the summer as the snow melts. The common name, Glacier Lily, comes from its characteristic of growing in the moist soil along the edges of snowbanks. As the snow melts, the soil is very wet. Glacier Lilies love wet soil and grow either in sunny meadows or partly shaded forests along edges of melting snow. Because they follow the snow line, they bloom earlier at lower elevations and move up the mountainside following the melting snow. Once all the snow has melted from an area and the ground dries up, these water lovers dry up too and their flowers turn to seeds.

**COLORFUL POLLEN** Pollen grains may be red or yellow on the dangling *anthers*. Look carefully to see the variations!

*family field guide*

### POLLINATORS

The drooping flower is most attractive to hummingbirds which hover below the flower and point their long beaks upward to sip the nectar. Bees are also attracted to Glacier Lily nectar.

### LEAVES AND STEMS

The leaves grow from the base of a single stem which supports a single flower.

### DISTINCTIVE DROOP

The flower appears too big for the delicate stem to hold it upright! Flowers that droop down this way are often designed to attract hummingbirds.

**Leaves** Two or three leaves grow up from the bottom of each plant.

**Habitat** Glacier Lilies grow in colonies where snow has recently melted and the soil is soggy.

# Monkeyflower

## Snapdragon Family

*Mimulus guttatus*

**ROCKY MOUNTAIN RELATIVES**
Louseworts, Paintbrushes, Penstemons

**EASY IDENTIFICATION**
Yellow flower with red spots; grow near water

**Flower** Some say the side view looks like a monkey with its lips sticking out.

**NAMES** The genus name *Mimulus* is Latin for "buffoon" and is the root of the common name Monkeyflower. Some say that the side-view of the flower looks like a monkey with big lips (see photo below). The species name *guttatus* is Latin for "speck" or "drop" and refers to the red dots on the flower.

**FANCY FERTILIZATION** *Fertilization* occurs when a male cell (pollen) touches a female cell (egg) and the egg starts to grow into a seed. In Monkeyflowers, the eggs are attached to the inside top of the flower and are contained in the female part called the *pistil*. Monkeyflower pistils have a unique shaped as a two-part "mouth" that closes when touched. Bees land on the lower lip of the flower, then they follow the red spots to the nectar. As they crawl into the flower, their backs touch the pistil and the "mouths" close. If the bees had any pollen on their backs, the mouths collect it and the egg is *fertilized* and starts to grow a seed. These mouths that open and close, protect the eggs from the flower's own pollen grains and ensure that fertilization occurs from the pollen of another plant.

**RIPARIAN FLOWER** Monkeyflower cannot live more than a few feet away from water. If the roots of this flower dry out, the plant shrivels and dies. If you notice a colony of Monkeyflowers in the shade, far from any river, stream or pond, a spring must be bubbling up from the spot.

*family field guide*

## FOOD

Deer, elk, bighorn sheep and muskrat eat the flowers.

## RIPARIAN ROOTS

Plants need to "breathe" just like animals do. Oxygen, nitrogen, carbon dioxide and other gases move in and out of leaves and roots. These gases drift below ground through tiny spaces in the soil. However, in wet soil, water fills most of the spaces so there are few gases available for the roots. Most riparian plant roots are shallow and feathery which provide more surface area for better absorption. They also have more tiny holes in their leaves (*stomata*) which stay open almost all day long, allowing gases to move easily in and out of the leaves.

## HYDROPHYTES

This fancy word simply means plants that love water. *Hydro* is Latin for water (think of a hydrant) and *phyte* means "attracted to."

**Leaves** The leaves grow opposite each other and vary in size.

**Habitat** Monkeyflower grows along streams or other waterways.

# Mullein

## Snapdragon Family

### Verbascum thapsus

**ROCKY MOUNTAIN RELATIVES**
Monkeyflower, Paintbrushes, Penstemons

**EASY IDENTIFICATION**
Soft, fuzzy leaves; grow in dry soil

**Leaves** The leaves are fuzzy-soft and grow into a tall stalk in their second year.

**PIONEER** Mullein (pronounced Mullen) was brought over from Europe. It has become very successful in the Western United States because it grows in places where the soil is dug up and turned over. Mullein grows best with a lot of sunlight, so when other plants are removed, there is nothing to shade the ground and Mullein seeds grow rapidly. When roads are built or irrigation ditches dug and piles of dirt are left on the side, Mullein is one of the first plants to grow, so it is called a *pioneer species*.

**TWO-YEAR CYCLE** Mullein plants grow in a two-year cycle. The first year, they grow a cluster of fuzzy-soft leaves. By the second year, they have stored enough energy to produce a flower that grows as tall as a third grade student. After the flower fomrs and produces seeds, the stalk dries up and the plant dies.

**WINTER BIRD FEEDER** The tall flower stalks dry up in winter and remain standing. Seeds are stored within the dried flowers and are held nicely above the snow as a feeder for hungry birds.

**MEDICINE** The soft rabbit-ear leaves have long been used to help with asthma, bronchitis and dry coughs. People who suffer from winter coughing spells might collect and dry Mullein leaves, then boil them in water to make a tea. Be sure to collect the leaves from a clean site (not next to a highway or an old mine).

*family field guide*

## BUMBLING BEES

The flowers are shaped just right for bumble bees to crawl inside. Flies and butterflies also pollinate Mullein flowers.

## HUGE STALK

The flower stalk can grow up to six-feet tall. A study in 2005 discovered that taller plants are more likely to be pollinated than shorter plants.

## ONE SHOT

After the Mullein has stored energy for one year, it flowers the second year then dies.

## SOFT LEAVES

The velvety soft leaves are a finger's delight.

**Flower** Flowers grow at the top of the tall stalk and are a favorite of ants and bees.

**Dead Stalks** Dried stalks remain in the spring from the previous summer.

family field guide

# Oregon Grape

## Barberry Family

*Mahonia repens*

**ROCKY MOUNTAIN RELATIVES**
None

**EASY IDENTIFICATION**
Holly-shaped leaves; grow in dry, sunny environments; blue-colored berries in mid-summer

**Flower** Bright yellow flowers grow in spring and turn to berries in mid-summer.

**FIRST OBSERVATIONS** In 1806 Meriwether Lewis described Oregon Grape as follows: "There are two species of evergreen shrubs which I first met with at the grand rapids of the Columbia (River) and which I have since found in this neighbourhood also; they grow in rich dry ground...each point of their margins is armed with a thorn or spine." Naturally, this observation was recorded while exploring near present-day Oregon.

**SHRUBBY EVERGREEN** Oregon Grape keeps its green leaves all year long, though they turn red in response to cold weather in spring and fall. Like most evergreen plants, this one is very *hardy*: it can survive droughts, freezing temperatures, extreme heat and animal grazing. Because it is so hard to kill and it keeps a nice color in winter, many gardeners use it for landscaping.

**SEED DISPERSAL** Oregon grape produces small bunches of blue-colored berries in mid-summer. The bright blue bundles look similar to grapes, but these little fruits are not so juicy. The early season crop is an important food source for birds and rodents because most berries do not form until later in the summer. The animals eat the berries, digest the fruit, travel to distant places, then plant the seeds in new locations.

*family field guide*

A different species of Oregon Grape (*Mahonia aquifolium*) is Oregon's state flower.

## GROUND COVER

Oregon Grape is sometimes called Creeping Oregon Grape because it grows low to the ground and spreads slowly along the forest floor. This type of ground cover is very important for holding the soil and preventing erosion, especially in dry soils that erode easily.

## YELLOW INSIDE

Beneath the woody bark is a bright yellow layer which has long been used to treat liver problems. The chemical in this layer is called Barberine and is the namesake for the plant family, Barberry.

**Habitat** Oregon Grape grows in dry soil and their leaves turn red in cooler weather.

**Berries** Blue-colored berries form in mid-summer. They are edible, but very sour.

*family field guide*

# Aster

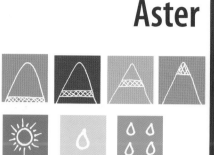

## Sunflower Family
### Aster Group

**ROCKY MOUNTAIN ASTERS**
Engelmann Aster, Subalpine Aster, Smooth Aster, Long-leaved Aster

**ROCKY MOUNTAIN DAISIES**
Aspen Daisy, Beautiful Daisy, Pinatteleaf Daisy, Subalpine Daisy

**EASY IDENTIFICATION**
Pink to white, daisy-shaped flowers

**Flower** Colors range from white to pink to purple.

**A TYPE OF ASTER** These purple and pink, daisy-shaped flowers are easy to identify within the Aster Group, but identifying the exact species of Aster or Daisy is very difficult. *Botany* is the official name for the study of flowers and *botanists* are trained to look at the small details of flowers. These details help determine a plant's identity, allow comparisons within plant families and in some cases help explain the evolution of the plant species. To precisely identify an Aster or Daisy, a naturalist must examine the habitat, leaves, blooming season, numbers of flowers per stem and other, more complicated flower details.

**SMALL DETAILS, BIG WORDS** Botonists use very big names to describe the small details of plants. It is obvious enough that a daisy-shaped, pink-petaled flower is identified within the Aster Group. Botanists, however, are suckers for details. Try understanding this comparison between two varieties of Tansy Aster as written by William Weber. "*M. bigelovii's* peduncles are very sticky; *M. canescens*' are not. Both *M. bigelovii* and *M. canescens* have phyllaries in overlapping rows with curved tips, but *M. bigelovii's* phyllaries are green at the tip and for at least half the length of the phyllary." Wow, with such tiny differences between species, it is no wonder that many amateur naturalists refer to purple or pink-petalled Daisies generically as "a type of Aster."

*family field guide*

## LATE SUMMER DISPLAY

Most Asters are very delicate plants that are easy to miss when growing individually. When growing in dense colonies, however, they create quite a colorful display in August.

## WORLDWIDE RELATIVES

There are over 600 different Aster species worldwide.

## GOOD EATIN'

Chipmunks and several birds eat the leaves and seeds; mule deer and rabbits eat the leaves only.

## LOOK CLOSELY

While identifying the different flowers within the aster group, Janis Huggins clearly distinguishes the differences between species in her book *Wild At Heart*. Be sure to use a hand lens when comparing flower species because the details that separate them are very small!

**Leaves** The leaves of different Asters vary and can be helpful in determining the species.

photo by National Park Service

**Habitat** Different types of Aster grow from the lowland shrub life zone up to the tundra.

*family field guide*

# Iris

## Iris Family

*Iris missouriensis*

**ROCKY MOUNTAIN RELATIVES**
None

**EASY IDENTIFICATION**
Unique flower

**Flower** The yellow signal patch leads bees into the flower where pollination occurs.

**A COLORFUL NAME** Iris is the name of the winged messenger of the gods in Greek mythology. She was the rainbow that extended from the heavens down to earth. The Iris plant was named after the colorful dress of this Greek messenger.

**POLLINATION** The purple and yellow lines and spots on the Iris petals attract bees and other insects, then guide them toward the nectar inside. As the insects crawl into the flower, their bodies are dusted with pollen. As they visit neighboring plants, the pollen on their bodies falls off and lands inside their female parts. When the pollen and eggs meet, a new seed will begin to grow. Pollination is a colorful act of nature.

**WET OR DRY?** Iris grow in wet, sunny meadows. They often grow in areas that appear dry, but the plant must have plenty of water up until the flower is formed. Once the flower is in bloom, the soil can dry out and the plant is not affected. If you see a clump of Iris growing in a dry meadow, know that it was a wet meadow weeks before.

**WHO NEEDS A SEED?** Iris usually grow in clusters of a dozen or so plants. The flowers produce seeds in large sturdy pods, but most colonies grow from *rhizomes*, underground stems which sprout new plants next to the original plant. Because these new plants grow from the same root system, all of the plants in a colony share the same food and water.

*family field guide*

## MISSOURI

The first Europeans collected and recorded this flower near the mouth of the Missouri River, thus the species name *missouriensis*.

## COLORS

Wild Iris range in color from deep to pale purple and sometimes nearly white. The color range is based on soil, moisture and, most of all, genetics.

## POISONOUS ROOTS

Iris roots are poisonous. Native Americans in the area may have ground up the roots and dipped their arrows into the potion to make their weapons more deadly.

## SEED POD

After the flower has been pollinated, it turns to a large seed pod filled with thousands of bee-bee-like seeds.

**Habitat** Iris grow well in open, sunny meadows that are still damp from melted snow.

**Leaves** Iris leaves are big and as tall as the stems. They often grow in clusters sharing the same roots.

# Larkspur

## Buttercup Family

*Delphinium barbeyi*
*Delphinium nuttalianum*

### ROCKY MOUNTAIN RELATIVES

Monkshood, Columbine, Pasque Flower, Red Columbine, Marsh Marigold

### EASY IDENTIFICATION

Flowers grow on a stalk and have a unique "spur"

**Flower** The name Larkspur comes from the "spur" that extends from the back .

**TWO TYPES** Two different types of Larkspur grow in the Rocky Mountains. Both have very similar flowers, but very different habitats, leaves and sizes. Subalpine Larkspur (*D. nuttalianum*) grows in lush meadows and sunny montane forests. It is often as tall as a third grader and has leaves as big as a third grader's hand. In contrast, Spring Larkspur (*D. barbeyi*) grows in dry, sun-baked lowlands, is rarely taller than a third grader's ankles and has leaves a bit larger than a quarter.

**POISON** Do not eat any type of Larkspur! Cattle may mistakenly eat these plants while grazing in the open range. If they eat more than 3% of their body weight they can die (equal to a 60 pound kid eating seven Quarter-Pounders worth of salad...not very likely, but it happens).

**ASPEN BEAUTY** Subalpine Larkspur grow alongside the white banners of Cow Parsnip in moist, sunny aspen groves. They bloom in mid-summer and create one of the most dramatic wildflower displays of all Rocky Mountain flower communities.

**RARE BEAUTIES** Occasionally Larkspur flowers are pure white or such a pale purple that they appear white. These rare beauties are sure to make you look twice and wonder if albinos exist within the plant kingdom. The color variation depends on soil and genetics.

*family field guide*

## BIG FAMILY

While two species of Larkspur grow in Colorado's Rocky Mountains, there are over 250 different plants within the genus Delphinium worldwide.

## LEAVES

Though the flowers of these two Larkspur plants are similar, the leaves are very different. Spring Larkspur (left) has a delicate leaf the size of a quarter which stores water better in the dry environment where it lives. Subalpine Larkspur leaves (right) are as large as a child's hand.

## NAMES

Delphinium is Latin for "dolphin" referring to the shape of the flowers just before they open.

**Spring Larkspur** Blooms in early summer and grows ankle-high in hot, dry conditions.

**Subalpine Larkspur** Blooms in mid-summer and grows tall in partial sunlight and moist soil.

# Lupine

## Pea Family

*Lupinus argenteus*

**ROCKY MOUNTAIN RELATIVES**
Alfalfa, Clover, Vetch

**EASY IDENTIFICATION**
Unique leaf; seed pods in late summer

**Flower** Many small flowers grow along the top of a tall slender stalk.

**WOLF FLOWER** The name Lupine comes from the Latin word *lupus* which means "wolf." Some say this name was given because the plant was thought to rob the soil of its minerals in the same way a wolf robs a shepherd of its sheep. Lupine is able to grow in sandy areas, so people long ago assumed that the plant was stealing nutrients from the soil leaving only sand in its place. In reality, Lupines and all members of the Pea Family, improve the soil.

**NITROGEN FIXATION** All plants need nitrogen to grow. Unfortunately when leaves, twigs or animals decompose, they do not replace nitrogen in the soil. If plants continue to "eat" nitrogen without replacing it, the soil can no longer support plant life. A special bacteria grows on the roots of Lupine, Clover, Alfalfa, Peas and all plants within the Pea Family that collects nitrogen from the air, mixes it with oxygen and makes it usable for other plants. Without these bacteria, nitrogen would simply drift through the soil without ever being used. Authors Raven, Evert and Curtis state in their book *Biology of Plants* that, "If the nitrogen that is removed from the soil were not steadily replaced, virtually all life on this planet would slowly disappear." For this reason, farmers have planted peas in their fields for thousands of years to help improve the output of their food crops.

*family field guide*

## PEA FAMILY

There are over 13,000 different species in the Pea Family. Some favorites include peanuts, soybeans, lentils and beans.

## PASS ME BY

Once a flower on the stalk has been pollinated its upper petal turns deep purple. This is a sign to bees that they can fly on by since the job has already been done.

## STATE FLOWER

A different species of Lupine (*Lupinus texensis*) is the state flower of Texas where they are called Bluebonnets.

## NOT FOR EATING

Many plants in the pea family are planted for food. Even Alfalfa and Clover are planted as food for cattle. Don't try eating Lupine though, this is not a trail snack.

**Leaf** Lupine leaves are unique with all the leaflets growing out from the center.

**Seeds** After the flower matures, it turns into a seed pod as do all plants in the Pea Family.

# Monkshood

## Buttercup Family

*Aconitum columbianum*

**ROCKY MOUNTAIN RELATIVES**
Columbine, Red Columbine, Larkspur

**EASY IDENTIFICATION**
Unique flower shape; grow in wet areas

photo by National Park Service

**Flower** The name Monkshood refers to the top petal which looks very much like a hood.

**POISON** Monkshood is one of the most poisonous plants in the Rocky Mountain region. A chemical called Aconitine collects in the roots in late fall when the plants are storing energy to survive underground through the winter. This poisonous chemical was used to poison enemy water supplies during times of war in ancient Europe and Asia. Hunters used the sap to poison spears and arrowheads as well.

**WATER LOVER** Monkshood grows in partial sun often along stream banks and beneath Aspen groves. They are very easy to see because they often grow up to six feet tall, which is taller than many adults!

**BEAUTY IS SKIN DEEP** The common name and scientific names reflect the contrast between Monkshood's beautiful appearance and its toxic chemistry. The common name Monkshood refers to the shape of the flower which appears like a hood as it folds over the top of the blossom. This religious reference contrasts with the scientific name which refers to the poisonous chemicals stored in the plant. The flower is very beautiful in its appearance, but it is one of the most dangerous plants in the region.

**UNIQUE FLOWER, COMMON LEAF** The Monkshood flower is easy to identify because it is so unique. The leaf, however, is so similar to Larkspur and Geranium that the plant is difficult to identify before the flowers bloom.

*family field guide*

## SEED POD

After the flowers are pollinated, tiny seed pods form in place of the flowers.

## HIDING

Monkshood is often overlooked because its deep purple flowers do not stand out brightly against the dark green leaves. Also, this plant grows in the same environment as Larkspur which has similar leaves and flower color, so the two are often mistaken for each other. Given a careful look at the flower, however, the two are very easy to distinguish.

## FLOWER SHAPE

The Monkshood shape is perfect for a bumblebee to climb right under the hood and into the flower. Bees are the primary pollinators.

**Leaf** The leaves are as large as a hand and are similar to Geranium and Larkspur leaves.

**Habitat** Monkshood grows up to six feet tall in wet areas and around stream beds.

# Penstemon

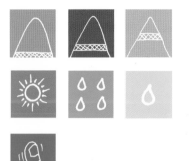

## Snapdragon Family

### Penstemon Group

**ROCKY MOUNTAIN VARIETIES**
Whipple's, Smooth, Rocky Mountain, and
Mat Penstomon and Osterhouts Beardtongue

**EASY IDENTIFICATION**
Two lips on top of the flower, three lips on
the bottom; many different species have this
similar flower shape

**Flower** All Penstemon flowers have two lips
on the top and three on the bottom

**MANY TYPES, SIMILAR FLOWER** There are over 250
different species of Penstemon in North America making this the most diverse of all plant groups on the con-
tinent. They vary from delicate flowers to large shrubs,
but all have very similar looking flowers with two upper lips, three lower lips and a central opening perfect
for hungry bumble-bees and hummingbirds.

**FREE REFILLS** A study in 2002 suggests that some
Penstemon species are able to control the amount of
nectar they produce. When the nectar of a Penstemon plant was removed once in six hours, the flower
refilled the amount that was removed. When nectar
was removed from the same flower every hour, the
plant refilled more than twice the amount of the first
trial. This experiment proves that the flower is able to
control the amount of nectar it produces based on how
much is used so that it will not go dry. By keeping its
nectar supply full, the flower can continuously attract
bees or hummingbirds, depending on the species.

**BUMBLING BEES** When bees enter a flower, pollen dusts their heads and bellies, but much of it falls
off when they clean themselves. Therefore, bee-pol-
linated Penstemon release a small amount of pollen
at a time so that it is not wasted by clumsy bees. It is
better for the plant to dust a little bit of pollen on a
lot of bees rather than placing a lot of pollen on a few
clumsy bees.

*family field guide*

## POLLINATION EVOLUTION

Some Penstemon species are shaped to attract bees while others are shaped to attract hummingbirds. Theories suggest that "bee flowers" evolved over time to become "bird flowers." After bees visit a flower, they often groom themselves, knock off the pollen and do not transfer pollen as efficiently as birds. Hummingbirds, however, fly from flower to flower without stopping and are better pollinators. Therefore, plants that attracted birds were pollinated more frequently, produced more seeds, then more flowers. Over millions of years, some species changed their shape to attract hummingbirds rather than bees.

**Hummers** Some Penstemon flowers droop downward and are designed for hummingbird pollination.

**Bees** Purple flowers are usually designed for bee pollination.

*family field guide*

# Silky Phacelia
## (Fringed or Alpine Phacelia)

## *Waterleaf Family*

### *Phacelia sericea*

**ROCKY MOUNTAIN RELATIVES**
Scorpionweed and Ball-head Waterleaf

**EASY IDENTIFICATION**
Gold pollen grains on purple flower; grow above treeline

**Flower** Gold pollen grains stand out from the purple flowers for easy identification.

**ALPINE ADAPTATIONS** Silky Phacelia grows very well in harsh conditions, especially in dry sandy soil in the alpine tundra life zone. To survive the dry conditions, this plant has a long taproot that may grow more than a foot into the soil where it can absorb water and nutrients. This adaptation of growing in rocky, sandy soil helps the plant stay warm because these rocky areas absorb more heat than grassy meadows. However, warm sand is not enough to combat the harsh conditions in the tundra, so the leaves have short hairs which protect against wind. Each tiny hair covers a small opening in the leaf so that the water does not get blown out of the plant. These hairs, or perhaps the silky look of the bright gold pollen grains, are the reason for the names Silky and Fringed Phacelia.

**NAME** The word Phacelia comes from a Greek word which means "bundles." The taproot of each plant most always grows bundles of several flowers in a dense cluster. This clustering characteristic helps protect the plant from harsh winds; the front flowers shield the back flowers from wind.

**GOLDEN SPECKS** Bright gold pollen grains are attached to long *anthers*, the male part of the plant. These golden attachments act like billboards attracting passing butterflies, bees and moths to land on the attractive flower.

*family field guide*

## TAP ROOT

Phacelia's roots dig deep into the sandy soil to anchor the plant against gusting winds and to absorb water from deep in the ground.

## ALPINE ADAPTED

Larger leaves grow at the base of the flower where wind cannot blow water out of them. Leaves higher up on the plant are much smaller.

**Habitat** Silky Phacelia grows best in dry rocky soil in the alpine tundra.

**Leaf** These leaves have protective hairs which act as shields against the wind.

# Sky Pilot
## (Sticky Jacob's Ladder)

## Phlox Family

*Polemonium viscosum*

**ROCKY MOUNTAIN RELATIVES**
Scarlet Gilia, Jacob's Ladder

**EASY IDENTIFICATION**
Many small *leaflets* growing opposite each other; orange pollen grains; grow in rocky soil of alpine meadows

**Flower** Bright orange pollen grains and white filaments lead bees to the nectar.

**SKUNKY SMELL** To get the full affect of a Sky Pilot, poke your nose close to the flower and inhale. In most cases they have a "skunky" smell; not the sweet smell that most people find attractive. Flies, however, love it! Occasionally, these flowers produce a sweeter smell, but scientists have observed that flies usually pass by the sweeter smelling flowers in favor of the skunky scent. Bees, however, prefer the sweet scented flowers.

**POLLINATION** Flies are first attracted to Sky Pilot flowers by the scent. As they hover over the flower, the bright orange pollen grains attract them further. Upon landing on the flower, they drag their feet through the pollen and follow the white lines down to the nectar. As they crawl over the flowers, the pollen which collects on their feet is dragged onto the female part (*pistil*), it drops onto the eggs inside and a new seed begins to grow.

**LIFE ON THE ROCKS** Sky Pilot grows in alpine tundra regions, usually in fields of small rocks called *scree fields* or fields of larger rocks called *talus slopes*. Scree fields do not appear to provide very good soil, but they are just the place that Sky Pilot likes to grow. A single deep taproot burrows deep below ground to get water and soil nutrients. Often, the plants cluster around gopher burrows where the soil is stirred up thus creating excellent growing conditions.

*family field guide*

## COLD MOUNTAIN PLANT

Clusters of bright flowers grow from hairy stems which rarely grow taller than a person's ankle.

## NAME

The Latin name *viscosum* means sticky. Rub the leaves and notice the sticky texture.

## LEAFLETS

Many small *leaflets* line a stem making a single compound leaf. The small leaflets are an adaptation to growing in the windy alpine tundra. When the wind blows past a leaf, it pulls water out of the plant. These tiny leaves provide a small surface from which the Sky Pilot can lose water.

**Leaf** Many small *leaflets* line each stem. These leaflets hold water better than large leaves.

**Habitat** Sky Pilots grow in rocky soil in the alpine tundra, especially in *scree fields* and *talus slopes*.

family field guide

# Blue Flax
## (Wild Blue Flax)

## Flax Family

*Linum lewisii*

**ROCKY MOUNTAIN RELATIVES**
None

**EASY IDENTIFICATION**
Delicate blue flowers; grow in clumps in hot, dry, sandy places

**Flower** The yellow spot in the middle attracts flies and bees to the flower.

**FIRST EXPLORATIONS** Meriwether Lewis was the first European to observe Wild Blue Flax and he looked at it with an interested eye. Two very important products, linen (used to make fabric) and flax oil, were produced from a species of Flax in the Eastern U.S. The eastern plants, however, were *annuals* that grow for one year then die. He hoped that this plant which appeared to grow back each year (*perennial*), would produce quality fibers and oil and that it would not need to be planted each year. After a year of experimentation, he discovered that this species does not produce quality fibers or oil, but it is used today as a colorful spring addition in peoples' gardens.

**ONE DAY ONLY** Each Flax flower lasts only one day. The flower opens in the morning, begins to close as the sun intensifies and falls off by evening. Fortunately dozens of flowers are in bloom at any one time and new flowers quickly replace those that drop, so the plant is never naked. As the flowers drop so quickly, so do new seeds which are spread abundantly to increase the chance of new plants germinating in the dry soil.

**HARDY PLANT** Wild Blue Flax looks fragile, but it grows well in harsh conditions. It's small leaves help to survive the heat. Water evaporates from leaves very quickly when temperatures are hot or when winds are constant. The small leaves do not provide much area for the sun to "pull" the water out of the plant.

*family field guide*

## INSECT ATTRACTION

A bright yellow center attracts flies and small bees to the bright golden pollen grains. Blue Flax is very low in nectar and does not attract bees very well, so flies are the most common pollinators. Bees, however, deposite pollen more effectively than flies, which clean themselves regularly, knocking the pollen grains off of their bodies. While flies are the most common pollinators, bees are the most effective pollinators.

## LONG-LASTING SEEDS

Flax seeds can survive in the soil for years before they grow. This allows them to wait until conditions are just right before *germinating* and allows a set of seeds to lie under the soil ready to grow after a fire.

## STICKY SEEDS

Flax seeds often fall on bare ground where they could be blown or washed away quite easily. These clever seeds, however, are coated with a sticky, jello-like substance which sticks to the soil when wet.

## NAME

The Latin name *Linum* refers to the Flax Family's importance in producing linen. The name *lewisii* is for Meriwether Lewis, the first European to collect this plant.

**Leaf** The leaves are tiny so little or no water evaporates on hot days.

**Habitat** Blue Flax is adapted to grow where it is hot, dry and sandy.

# Bluebells
## (Mountain Bluebells)

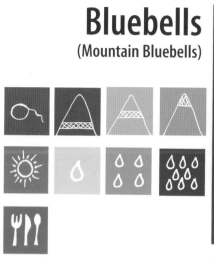

, ## *Borage Family*

### *Mertensia ciliata*

**ROCKY MOUNTAIN RELATIVES**
Forget-Me-Nots, Houndstongue

**EASY IDENTIFICATION**
Blue bell-shaped flowers hang downward

**Flower** The delicate bell-shaped flowers hang downward from their stems.

**THEY'RE EVERYWHERE** No matter where you are in the Rocky Mountains, you are likely to see this common flower. Five different species of Bluebells grow in the Rocky Mountains. Two species, *M. ciliata* and *M. franciscana*, grow as tall bushy plants with hundreds of flowers along streambanks in Aspen groves and Spruce-Fir forests; they grow knee-high along streambanks above treeline. Close cousins *M. lanceolata* and *M. brevistyla* grow in moist sunny meadows far from any stream. A little brother called Dwarf Bluebell (*M. fusiforma*) grows ankle-high in dry, sandy soil in the lowland shrub ecosystem. All species of Bluebells have the same flower shape, but each has a different leaf and grows in different conditions.

**TRAIL SNACKS** Some people like to snack on the blue-green leaves of Mountain Bluebells (*M. ciliata*). Janis Huggins describes the flavor as oyster-like in her book *Wild at Heart*. The texture is smooth and there is a lot of substance to the leaf making it an enjoyable addition to garden salads or a trail snack while out exploring. Deer, elk, bear and pika enjoy the leaves too!

**BLUE-GREEN LEAVES** Some Bluebells are easy to identify by their leaves. The species *ciliata* has blue-green leaves that differ from other plants in wet, boggy areas.

*family field guide*

## MOST COMMON

*Mertensia ciliata* is the most common Bluebell species in the western United States.

## LIGHT BRIGHT

Sometimes the color of these flowers is so bright, they look like a fluorescent light bulb glowing through a dangling blue lampshade.

## POLLINATORS

These bright blue flowers are very attractive to bees and the shape is perfect for them to crawl inside. Some flowers are too narrow for queen bees to reach all the way to the nectar and so worker bees tend to be the most common pollinators.

## DIFFERENCES

*Ciliata* and *franciscana* both grow in moist soil and along stream banks and grow as large bushes or in dense colonies. *Ciliata* has blue-green leaves; *franciscana* has bright green leaves.

*Brevistyla and lanceolata* both grow ankle-high in dry, sandy soil. Both grow as single plants, not huge bushes like the species mentioned above. *Brevistyla* has hairy top leaves, *lanceolata* has smooth leaves.

*Fusiforma* grows ankle-high as a single plant in dry, sandy soil.

**Leaf** Leaves vary between species. *M. ciliata* (above) is blue-green, others are bright green.

**Habitat** Bluebells grow in many different habitats, ranging from stream banks to dry hillsides.

# Columbine
## (Colorado Blue Columbine)

## Buttercup Family

### Aquilegia coerulea

---

**ROCKY MOUNTAIN RELATIVES**
Red Columbine, Marsh Marigold, Larkspur, Monkshood and more

---

**EASY IDENTIFICATION**
Unique flower with five spurs; grow in sunny aspen forests and alpine meadows

**Flower** Columbine flowers have long "spurs," bright pollen grains and white petals.

**SPURS** The Latin name *Aquilegia* refers either to the Latin word for "eagle" (Aquila) or for "water collector." Both definitions refer to the talon-like spurs which flare off the back of the flower and store nectar.

**HUMMERS AND HAWK MOTHS** Hummingbirds and huge moths called hawk or sphynx moths are attracted to Columbine nectar. Both have long "tongues" that reach deep into the spurs. Hummingbirds prefer the flowers that droop downward so that they can reach up to the flower, hawk moths prefer flowers that face upward, so they can hover above the flowers when drinking.

**SEPALS AND PETALS** When people think of a flower, they picture bright petals. Flower petals are usually colorful to attract insects. Columbine, however, have five white petals in the center of the flower which flare backward to form five nectar cups or "spurs." Spaced between each white petal is a blue or purple part called a *sepal* that looks like a petal. The sepal's main job is to surround the eggs and help protect the inside parts of the flower and it is usually green in color. Columbine are unusual because the blue sepals are bright and equally as attractive as the petals.

**STATE FLOWER** Colorado state law prohibits uprooting this, Colorado's state flower, from public lands! This law allows generations of people to admire this beautiful flower species.

*family field guide*

## SUN LOVER

Colorado's state flower grows from sunny aspen groves to moist alpine meadows.

## CONFLICTING NAMES

The name Columbine means "dove" (some say the back view looks like a dove) and the scientific name refers to an eagle. One is a bird of peace, the other a bird of prey.

## BUSHES

In alpine meadows Columbine grow as small, shin-high flowers, but in aspen groves they can grow as large, knee-high bushes.

**Leaf** Columbine leaves are delicate, but abundant, making a bushy plant below the flowers.

**Habitat** Columbine flowers like sunshine and commonly grow in open meadows.

# Clover
## (Red Clover)

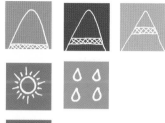

# Pea Family

*Trifolium pratense*

**ROCKY MOUNTAIN RELATIVES**
Alfalfa, Lupine, Vetches, Locoweed

**EASY IDENTIFICATION**
Leaves in clusters of three; pink/white flower cluster; grow in open meadows

**Flowers** The pink flowers grow like the top of a Q-Tip.

**FLOWER OF THE FIELDS** Clover has always been planted by farmers as food for cattle and chickens. Leftover plants which are not used as food are plowed into the soil as a natural fertilizer. Many fertilizers are high in nitrogen and while Clover does not have nitrogen in it, a fungus grows on its roots that collects nitrogen from the air and makes it usable for all plants.

**NAME** The common name "clover" refers to the club that Hercules carried which was known as 'clave trinodis.' It was said to have been a tree trunk with three large roots. The clover shape on playing cards which we call "clubs" refers to Hercules' club as well.

**TASTY TREAT** Clover flowers were once called "honeysuckle" because they were sweet enough to suck on. Since refined sugar has changed the meaning of "sweet," Clover no longer satisfies most sweet cravings, but bees and butterflies still flock to the nectar-filled flowers. The leaves and stems are also edible and are a natural addition to salads.

**NON-NATIVE** Clover was brought to the United States from Europe by farmers long ago. It grows well in sunny meadows, pastures, sidewalk cracks and empty lots. It often grows amidst a tangle of other grasses, but the two-toned leaves are easy to identify and the flowers bloom throughout the summer. Though Clover is not a native plant, it is not considered an *invasive* weed.

*family field guide*

## NOT A WEED

While clover is not a native plant it is not considered an *invasive* weed. It maintains a good reputation because it helps farmers and native plant communities by improving the usable nitrogen in soil. Also it does not grow so aggressively that it replaces native plants.

## TWO-TONED LEAVES

Clover is easy to identify by the light patches on its rounded leaves.

**Stems** Clover stems are long and tangly like a vine.

**Leaf** The genus name *Trifolium* means "three leaves."

# Elephant-head
## (Elephantella)

## Snapdragon Family
### Pedicularis groenlandica

**ROCKY MOUNTAIN RELATIVES**
Louseworts, Mullein, Monkeyflower, Paintbrushes, Penstemons

**EASY IDENTIFICATION**
Fern-like leaves; unique flowers; grow in sunny, wet meadows

**Flower** Many flowers grow on the flower stalk; each has a trunk and two ears.

**A THOUSAND HEADS** These bright pink flower stalks contain dozens of tiny pink flowers. Look closely at each little flower and notice the "trunk" and two "ears" that look like an elephant's head!

**LICE** While the common name refers to the largest land mammal on earth (the elephant), the genus name refers to one of the smallest: lice. *Pediculus* is Latin for "lice". It was once thought that cows who ate any plants of this genus (there are six in Colorado's Rocky Mountains) would become infested with lice. The generic name for this genus is "Lousewort."

**HEMIPARASITE** Elephant-head plants are *hemiparasites* or semi-parasites. *Hemi* means partly and a *parasite* is a living thing that steals nutrients from another living thing. While Elephant-heads can make their own food through photosynthesis, they also tap into roots of other plants and steal their nutrients and some of their chemical defenses. Small tissues reach from Elephant-head roots, dig into the roots of neighboring plants and, like a vacuum, suck water and nutrients from the other plant. Elephant-head is known to steal nutrients from a flower called Arrowleaf Groundsel, which is poisonous. The Elephant-head in return, steals the poisonous chemicals from the Groundsel making it less attractive to animals!

## GREENLAND

The species name *groelandica* refers to Greenland. Surprisingly, this plant no longer grows there.

## WET AND MUSHY

Elephant-heads grow in full sunlight and need lots of water. They are only found in sunny subalpine and alpine meadows that are wet and marshy.

## FERNY LEAF

Even before the flowers bloom, Elephant-heads are easy to identify by their ferny leaves. The small *leaflets* do not allow water to be blown out of the plant by gusty alpine winds.

**Leaf** Elephant-head leaves look like ferns with small leaflets growing opposite each other.

**Habitat** Elephant-heads grow in damp soil and sunny high-mountain meadows.

# Fairyslipper
## (Calypso Orchid)

## Orchid Family

*Calypso bulbosa*

**ROCKY MOUNTAIN RELATIVES**
Bog Orchid, Striped Coralroot Orchid

**EASY IDENTIFICATION**
Unique flower; hard-to-see leaves; grow in Lodgepole Pine forests

**Flower** The crown of petals and beautiful colors make this a uniquely beautiful flower.

**MYTHICAL BEAUTY** In the classic story *The Odyssey*, Calypso was queen of her own remote island. She was so beautiful that the hero of the story, Odysseus, was hypnotized by her beauty and remained on her island for seven years. There are several similarities between the queen and the flower: they are both rare and difficult to find, they both live in very specific locations and they are both uniquely beautiful.

**NOTHING TO OFFER** This colorful flower attracts hungry bees, but it does not produce nectar. Young bees that haven't yet learned to avoid this "useless" flower land on the bottom "lip" of the flower then follow the stripes and spots to the flower's center. Following a short exploration of the flower, the bees realize there is no nectar and they leave the plant with pollen dusted on their bodies. The young bees continue to explore several dozen other Fairyslippers before realizing that this orchid is a waste of time. In the process several dozen flowers are pollinated and new seeds are formed.

**FUNGAL NEIGHBOR** Fairyslippers, and many other orchids, only grow alongside a specific fungus in the soil. Orchid seeds are very small and contain few nutrients; the fungus provide sugars and minerals that allow the seed to sprout. Don't try to transplant a Fairyslipper because killing or eliminating the fungus in the soil will kill the flower, too!

*family field guide*

## AUTHOR'S CHOICE

These flowers are favorite spring and early summer discoveries. They are not common, are small and easy to miss and are delicately beautiful.

## ONE STEM, ONE LEAF, ONE FLOWER

A single leaf grows at the very bottom of the single stem which holds up the head of a single flower.

## LODGEPOLE PINES

These delicate flowers are almost always found growing in Lodgepole Pine forests. Needles fall off the pine trees and land on the forest floor making a mat of dried needles called *duff*. The duff layer holds in water and shades the ground creating a perfect environment for white strands of fungus to grow beneath the wet soil. Fairyslipper seeds need this fungus to germinate.

**Habitat** Fairyslippers grow in a blanket of forest litter, commonly in Lodgepole Pine forests.

**Colonies** When conditions are right, Fairyslippers can grow in small colonies.

# Fireweed

*Evening Primrose Family*

*Chamerion angustifolium*

## ROCKY MOUNTAIN RELATIVES
Stemless Evening-Primrose

## EASY IDENTIFICATION
Clusters of pink flowers on tall stems; grow in sunny meadows

**Flower** Many delicate flowers grow on the flower stalk.

**PIONEER FLOWER** Like Aspen and Lodgepole Pine, Fireweed is a *pioneer species*. Following an avalanche, fire, construction or any disturbance, Fireweed is one of the first plants to grow in the unvegetated soil. This flower loves full sunlight. It spreads quickly from underground stems called *rhizomes* that send up new flowers next to the parent plant. This fast growth is important following a disturbance because the roots hold the soil in place preventing erosion and allow slower-growing plants to mature.

**SLOW OPENING** Dozens of pink flowers grow from a single Fireweed stem. It is very difficult to find a Fireweed stalk with all of the blossoms open at the same time! The bottom flowers open first, then, as they become pollinated, the flowers towards the top open. Bees are very attracted to Fireweed nectar and rub the pollen off of a few flowers on the plant, then they fly to a neighboring plant to find more blooming flowers. By forcing the bee to fly to a neighboring plant, the bee is less likely to pollinate a flower on the same stalk. The characteristic of plants opening only a few flowers at a time is called *potandry*.

**FEATHERY SEEDS** After the flowers have all dried up, the Fireweed stalk becomes a tangle of feathery seeds waiting to blow away on the wind.

*family field guide*

## SEEDS

Fluffy, cottony seeds form in late summer. Up to 80,000 seeds are produced on a single plant!

## NECTAR

Fireweed is very attractive to bees because it is one of the most nectar-rich flowers in the region.

**Leaf** Long, thin leaves with an obvious main vein grow outward from the stem.

**Habitat** Fireweed grows in sunny areas that have been disturbed by fire, avalanche or construction.

# Moss Campion

## Pink Family

*Silene acaulis*

**ROCKY MOUNTAIN RELATIVES**
Chickweeds, Sandworts, White Campion

**EASY IDENTIFICATION**
Small pink flowers; cushion of leaves no more than 2 inches tall; grow only in alpine tundra

**Cushion Plant** The cluster of leaves and woody stems form a cushion.

**ALPINE ADAPTATIONS** Moss Campion grows only in the alpine tundra and only as tall as a pinky finger. By staying low to the ground, it avoids strong winds and is able to absorb warmth from the ground. The leaves are very small so that wind does not pull water from them. It grows in the rockiest soils and on cliff ledges from a single root 4-5 feet deep which secures the plant. The depth of the roots also provides access to water and nutrients. Even with these adaptations, a Moss Campion may require over 25 years to grow to the size of a dinner plate!

**SOIL CATCHER** Wind gusts in the alpine tundra are extremely strong during big storms. Any soil that is not held down by plant roots is likely to blow away. As small bits of soil blow across the ground, they often get caught in the tangle of Moss Campion leaves. When this happens, Moss Campion grows slightly taller as it adds soil to its cushion of leaves and it prevents additional soil from blowing away.

**WATCH YOUR STEP** Plants in the alpine tundra only have three months to grow each year. If someone steps on a Moss Campion or other high alpine plant it can cause the plant to use a season's energy supply repairing broken leaves or branches rather than producing flowers or growing larger. Therefore it is important to step carefully and stay on trails at all times when exploring in the alpine life zone.

*family field guide*

## SHORT GROWING SEASON

Plants can grow only when temperatures are warm enough for water to flow through the roots, stems and leaves. In the alpine tundra, plants are only able to grow for 2-3 months each year. Plants lower on the mountain may have an extra month or two to grow.

## NOT A MOSS

The name Moss Campion can be misleading. This plant is not a moss at all. Mosses do not produce flowers or seeds. Instead, they produce spores which must land in water to form new plants. Moss Campion does produce flowers and requires insects to spread pollen to the eggs to form new seeds.

**Leaf** The leaves are tiny to prevent wind from pulling water out of the plant.

**Flower** The pink flowers are small, but very outstanding against the green leaves.

# Parry's Primrose

## Primrose Family

### Primula parryi

**ROCKY MOUNTAIN RELATIVES**
Northern Rock Jasmine

**EASY IDENTIFICATION**
Obvious pink flowers; grow in wet, sunny meadows

**Flower** The brilliant pink flowers stand out amongst all neighboring flowers.

**CHARLES PARRY** Charles Parry was an English doctor who worked and lived in Iowa, but he liked to spend most of his time studying and enjoying nature. He was the first European to collect and describe several plants. Mr. Parry had the honor of naming Grey's Peak, one of the tallest mountains in Colorado, after his friend Asa Grey who was an explorer and botanist. In return, Mr. Grey named Parry's Primrose after the English doctor who lived in Iowa.

**STINKY BEAUTY** These flowers are brighter and the plant is larger than most alpine plants. Parry's Primrose is a photographer's dream with brilliant pink petals, a yellow center and neon green leaves. But, get too close to the flower and you'll notice the odor. The beautiful flower attracts people, but the smell attracts the flies that pollinate it.

**PROTECTION** Most plants that live in the tundra grow low to the ground, have small leaves and hairs that protect them from water loss. However, Parry's Primrose grows tall, has large leaves and none of the normal adaptations for surviving the cold. Its secret lies in growing in shallow depressions, below stream banks, on the protected-side of rock ledges and other areas where it remains out of the wind. Even though it hides behind windbreaks, Parry's Primrose is easy to locate because its flowers are so bright.

*family field guide*

## WATER LOVER

This tall plant loves sunshine and water. It grows only in boggy subalpine and alpine meadows and along the edges of open stream banks and waterfalls.

## NAME

The Latin word *Primula* means "early spring." Parry's Primrose blooms shortly after the snow melts when the soil is still wet. Winter is much longer in the subalpine and alpine life zones than at lower elevations, so "early spring" does not occur for this flower until July or even August!

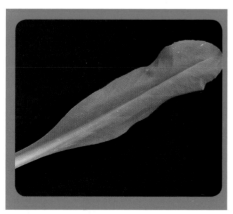

**Leaf** The leaf is nearly as long as the flower is tall and is smooth and rounded at the top.

**Habitat** Pink blossoms are very obvious around lakes, bogs or wet depressions in the alpine tundra.

# Thistle

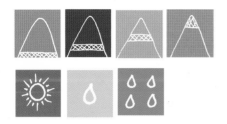

## Sunflower Family

### Thistle Group

**NATIVE THISTLES**
Aspen Thistle, Eaton's Thistle, Elk Thistle
Mountain Thistle, Parry's Thistle and more

**INVASIVE THISTLES**
Canada, Plumeless and Musk Thistles

**EASY IDENTIFICATION**
Thorny leaves and stems; grow in sunny areas

**Elk Thistle** This native thistle grows in high mountain meadows and is not a weed.

**NATIVES AND NON-NATIVES** Fifteen different species of thistle are *native* to this region. These native-plants are important food for butterflies and other insects and they live in dry, rocky places where other plants cannot survive. Several different species of thistle were brought here from Europe; these plants are called *non-native*, or *introduced* species.

**INVASIVE SPECIES** Non-native thistles have a bad reputation because they grow so fast and reproduce so well that they prevent growth of native plants. They are called *invasive species* because they grow so aggressively that they invade the landscape. Invasive thistles include Plumeless, Musk and Canada Thistle.

**DUTY CALLS** Land owners in some counties are required by law to pull or spray invasive thistles on their property in an effort to control the spread of these non-native plants. If the land owner does not work to control them, the county hires people to do the work and the land owner has to pay the bill.

**WHAT'S THE DIFFERENCE?** It is sometimes difficult to know the difference between a native and a non-native plant. A first step is to look where the thistle is growing. If it is in the wilderness or near a forest, far from pastures, roads or construction, the plant is likely native. A thistle growing in or near a place that has recently been disturbed is likely a non-native weed.

*family field guide*

## SMART SEEDS

Many thistles produce pretty pink flowers. Once pollinated, these flowers turn to fluffy seeds that blow on the wind landing far from the parent. Canada Thistle can produce 1,000-5,000 seeds per plant.

## PRICKLY DEVILS

While it is important to pull non-native thistles before they form seeds, be sure to wear thick gloves to protect your hands from the prickly leaves and stems.

## CAREFUL PICKIN'

Pick Canada Thistle carefully. Picking the plant without pulling the root can make the plant grow larger. A broken root can cause more roots to grow, again making the plant larger. These plants are a real bugger and requre a combination of mowing, chemicals and biological controls. See the Colorado State Cooperative Extension website for details about how to control this invasive weed.

**Plumeless Thistle** These thorny weeds grow like small shrubs in dry, disturbed soil.

**Canada Thistle** Thorny leaves and stems grow tall and straight in moist soil.

# King's Crown

## Stonecrop Family
### Sedum integrifolium

**ROCKY MOUNTAIN RELATIVES**
Queen's Crown, Yellow Stonecrop

**EASY IDENTIFICATION**
Stiff leaves; maroon flower cluster; grow above treeline

**Flower** These unique maroon flowers are stiff and bristly.

**SUCCULENT** The leaves of King's Crown are thick and waxy. Plants with such leaves are called *succulents* and are built to store more water than other plants. Most succulents grow in the desert, but King's Crown has developed these special leaves to hold water in the windy alpine tundra. The leaf stores water and a waxy coating on the outside of the leaf stops water from leaving the leaf. Though King's Crown can grow in moist areas near streams or glacial lakes, it prefers sandy soil where water drains away from the plant quickly.

**FAST SPREADING** Woody roots extend out from the plant and new stems spread quickly through sandy soil. If you pick a stem close to the root, then replant it in moist soil nearby it will begin to grow roots within several days. This way of growing from cuttings is one type of *vegetative reproduction* in which new plants can grow without a seed.

**SUCCULENT ADAPTATIONS** Plants have tiny holes in their leaves called *stomata* which act like nostrils. Carbon dioxide and oxygen pass in and out of the plant through these tiny holes. Plants are able to control when these holes open and when they close. When the holes are open, water evaporates from the leaves. Most succulents open their stomata only at night when temperatures are cool; such timing is another way the plant minimizes evaporation through the leaves.

*family field guide*

## FALL COLORS

Besides the beautiful ruby-red blossoms which flower through the end of August, King's Crown leaves turn red in fall, creating a brilliant ground cover display where the plant has spread across the tundra floor.

## EROSION CONTROL

King's Crown spreads quickly across the sandy soil. Its roots hold soil in place preventing it from blowing away.

## SURVIVAL

Some say that the leaves can be chewed in a survival situation if a person is desperate for water. The leaves are also high in Vitamins A and C.

**Leaf** Small leaves are stiff and succulent. They store water in the dry alpine environment.

**Habitat** King's Crown ranges from dry rocky ledges to sunny meadows within the alpine tundra.

# Paintbrush

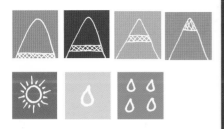

## Snapdragon Family
### Paintbrush Group

**ROCKY MOUNTAIN RELATIVES**
Monkeyflower, Pentemons, Louseworts

**EASY IDENTIFICATION**
Unique flower shape

**Flower** The green spines sticking out from this Narrowleaf Paintbrush are the flowers.

**ONE NAME, MANY FLOWERS** The name Indian Paintbrush refers to any flower in the genus *Castilleja* of which there are over 100 different species in the world. Each type of Paintbrush has a slightly different leaf and color and grows in a specific environment, but all Paintbrushes look similar enough to easily identify them.

**COLORFUL LEAVES** The brightly colored tops of the Paintbrush, which most people consider the flower, are actually very colorful leaves. The colored leaves at the top are a similar shape as the green leaves around the stem. The flower (that part which contains the pistil, stamen, pollen and ovary) is a tiny greenish tube which stands upright and barely sticks above the leaves when ready for pollination. Each plant supports several tiny flowers.

**HUMMERS AND PAINTBRUSH** Hummingbirds are attracted to bright colors, have almost no taste buds or sense of smell, but require a lot of sugary-sweet nectar to keep their wings hummin'. Indian Paintbrushes have very bright colors, but almost no scent at all and produce a lot of nectar. Because of these characteristics, scientists think that Indian Paintbrushes and hummingbirds have evolved to depend on each other; the hummers need the plants for food and the plants need the hummers for pollination. The process of two species evolving to depend on each other is called *coevolution*.

*family field guide*

## NATIVE AMERICAN STORY

This flower inspired the legend of an Indian brave who tried to paint the sunset with his war paints. Frustrated because he could not match the beauty of nature, he asked for guidance from the Great Spirit. The Great Spirit gave him paint brushes with all of the colors he desired. He painted his masterpiece with these paint brushes, then left them in the fields. According to the legend, the colorful flowers that we see today sprouted from these colorful paintbrushes.

## SEMI-PARASITIC

Indian Paintbrush produce their own food through photosynthesis, but also tap into the roots of neighboring plants to steal minerals and other nutrients.

## WYOMING STATE FLOWER

Narrowleaf Paintbrush (pictured at left) is Wyoming's state flower.

## TRAIL SNACKS

Pull one of the green tubes out from between the colorful leaves and nip off the bottom with your teeth. Enjoy the slight splash of nectar on your tongue (if you get to it before the birds).

## BIG RANGE

Indian Paintbrush grow from Alaska, south through Canada, the western United States, Central America and in the Andes of southern South America.

**Colors** Indian Paintbrush come in many colors including red, orange, pink and white, like this Sulfur Paintbrush.

**Habitat** Paintbrush grow in dry lowlands (pictured with Arrowleaf Balsamroot) and all life zones up to the alpine tundra.

# Red Columbine

## Buttercup Family

*Aquilegia elegantula*

**ROCKY MOUNTAIN RELATIVES**
Columbine, Monkshood, Larkspur

**EASY IDENTIFICATION**
Five red spurs point upward; yellow pollen grains hang downward

**Flower** The red flower hangs downward and its nectar is a favorite hummingbird food.

**MANY NAMES** Western Red Columbine, Comet Columbine and Shooting Star Columbine are all common names for this flower.

**HUMMINGBIRD FEEDERS** Hummingbirds love the Red Columbine. They are an important early season food source for hummingbirds arriving during their spring migration. Red Columbine nectar is 44% sugar while the Colorado Columbine is only 26% sugar. For comparison, the Red Columbine is like drinking 2 Cups of water with 1 Cup of Kool-Aid mx while the Colorado Columbine is like drinking the same amount of water with only $1/2$ Cup of Kool-Aid mix. Hummingbirds need a lot of energy to survive so they prefer the Red Columbine when it is available.

**HUMMINGBIRD SHAPE** Not only are Red Columbines filled with very sweet nectar, but their shape attracts the hummers, too. The flowers droop downward, requiring pollinators to hover below the flower and to tilt their heads upward to dip their beaks into the nectar spurs. Butterflies and moths prefer to hover above a flower while drinking, while hummingbirds prefer to hover below the flower and drink with their beaks tilted upward. Therefor, the drooping flowers of Red Columbines protect the nectar from butterflies and moths, saving it for hummingbirds. Also, by storing the nectar in the narrow little spurs, neither bees nor flies can access the sweet treat.

*family field guide*

## SURVIVOR

Red Columbine grow in montane forests which are prone to forest fires. This delicate flower grows from an underground stem six inches or so below the soil surface. When a fire burns quickly or passes high in the tree-tops, the underground stem is protected by the soil allowing Red Columbine to grow back after a mild burn.

## ELEGANT FLOWER

As the Latin name *elegantula* implies, the Red Columbine is a very elegant flower.

## COUSINS

There are 23 different species of Columbine around the world. Besides the five spurs which extend to the back of the flower and very similar leaves, Red Columbine and the Colorado Columbine look quite different. The Red Columbine flowers are about the size of a quarter, hang slightly downward and grow best in partly shaded forests while its cousin is the size of the palm of your hand, opens wide and faces directly into the full sun.

**Habitat** Red Columbine grow in the partial shade of evergreen forests.

**Leaf** The leaves are very similar those of Colorado Columbine.

# Scarlet Gilia

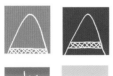

## *Phlox Family*
### *Ipomopsis aggregata*

**ROCKY MOUNTAIN RELATIVES**
Sky Pilot, Jacob's Ladder

**EASY IDENTIFICATION**
Red trumpet-shaped flowers at the tops of long delicate stems; grow in dry, sandy soil

**ONE SHOT** Scarlet Gilia grows for 1-8 years as a small bundle of leaves then, once it has stored enough energy, it sends up its tall stem and a season's array of flowers. After the flowers bloom and are pollinated, the entire plant dies, but not before dropping dozens of seeds beneath it.

**MAMMAL FOOD** Over half of all Scarlet Gilia stems are snipped and eaten by deer or elk. Fortunately for the Gilia, once the main stem is snipped, five new stems will grow and produce five times the number of flowers which in turn produce five times the number of seeds of a non-grazed plant. In this way, Scarlet Gilia actually benefits from animal grazing. The slender plant pictured above has not been grazed, but the bushy plant in the illustration has been grazed.

**LEAFY ADAPTATIONS** Plants that grow in the hot, drying sun have similar adaptations to plants growing in the windy alpine tundra. Tiny hairs grow on the leaves of Scarlet Gilia just as they do on many alpine plants. Leaves have tiny holes on them called *stomata* that allow gases to move in and out of the plant. If these holes are not shielded, water quickly evaporates in the hot sun or gusty wind. Plants in harsh environments also have small leaves which provide little area from which the sun or wind can pull water from the plant.

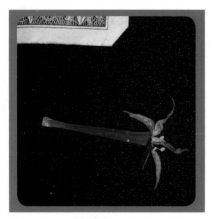

**Flower** The tube-like structure is inviting to hummingbirds and sphynx moths.

*family field guide*

## POLLINATORS

The Broad-tailed Hummingbird and White-lined Sphinx, a large moth with a "tongue" as long as a hummingbird's, feed from the trumpet-shaped flowers.

## EVERLASTING

Scarlet Gilia is commonly observed because it blooms from spring through late summer. It grows on sunny, dry hillsides including road embankments.

**Leaf** The tiny leaves are adapted to surviving very hot conditions.

**Habitat** Scarlet Gilia grows best in hot, dry environments with poor soil.

# Cattail

## Cattail Family

*Typha latifolia*

**ROCKY MOUNTAIN RELATIVES**
None

**EASY IDENTIFICATION**
Flower looks like a hot dog; grows in or near standing water

**Flower** The stick at the top makes pollen, the brown "hot dog" is a cluster of female flowers.

**POND PALS** Cattails grow in marshes and along pond edges in all fifty states. Their leaves and seeds are used as nesting material by birds, their leaves provide shade and protection for fish, frogs and salamanders. Cattail roots are a favorite food for muskrats while beavers use the leaves to patch holes in their dams. Cattail roots also provide erosion control by help hold the soil along lake edges and wetlands during flood seasons. Cattails serve many needs within the riparian ecosystem.

**BOYS AND GIRLS** Like all flowering plants, Cattails have boy parts and girl parts. The "hot dog" is the female flower which remains green and hidden by leaves in early spring. The boy part is a stick which grows from the top of the "hot dog"; this stick makes pollen in spring then falls off. Pollen blows from the sticks to neighboring green hot dogs. Once the pollen lands on the girl flowers, the flowers are *fertilized*, the green hot dog turns brown and the stick falls off. As the flower matures, the brown hot dog turns to a cluster of seeds that look very much like cotton candy on a stick.

**RHIZOMES** Though cattails have all the parts to make seeds, they most commonly reproduce through their roots. Underground stems called *rhizomes* grow from the parent plant, allowing many new plants to grow very close together. Cattail colonies can spread quickly through a wetland or bog without waiting for seeds to *germinate*.

*family field guide*

## PANCAKES

The spike at the top of the "hot dog" is the male part of the plant. It produces pollen in spring and lots of it! Some people collect the pollen in a bag and mix it with flour to make pancakes. The pollen is very nutritious and adds a nice flavor to morning flapjacks. Mix equal parts Cattail pollen and baking flour with a typical pancake recipe or use the one below:

$^1/_2$ Cup cattail pollen, $^1/_2$ Cup all purpose flour, 2 tsp. baking powder, 1 Cup milk, 1 egg, $^1/_4$ tsp. salt, 1 Tbsp. sugar, 2 Tbsp. oil

## FOUR SPECIES

There are only 4 species within the Cattail family. At least one species grows in every state of the USA. In contrast, there are over 24,000 species within the Sunflower Family.

**Seed** In fall , the Cattail seeds look like cotton candy on a stick.

**Habitat** Cattail grows best in or near still water, but do not grow well in flowing water.

# Corn Lily
## (False Hellebore)

# Lily Family
## *Veratrum californicum*

**ROCKY MOUNTAIN RELATIVES**
Mariposa Lily, Glacier Lily

**EASY IDENTIFICATION**
Unique leaves; grow in sunny, wet meadows

**Flower** Clusters of small white flowers grow at the top of a tall stalk.

**SPRING GROWTH** This unique plant grows very quickly in spring. Immediately as snow melts, when the ground is still wet, these green stalks grow 4-6 feet tall within several weeks. That means they grow 2-4 inches each day; fast-growing children may require a year or more to grow that much!

**BOGGY BOTTOMS** California Corn Lily grows best in wet, soggy soil. It grows in open sunny meadows or beneath the canopy of Aspen groves. Similar to the Aspen trees which often surround them, these leafy green giants also grow as *clones* from the same root system. The roots beneath Corn Lily colony are often one connected plant that is decades, sometimes hundreds of years old!

**BOYS AND GIRLS** Unlike most wildflowers, male Corn Lily plants produce pollen and separate female plants carry eggs. A grove growing from a single root then, has all male or all female plants, not a combination of both. This fact reveals a disadvantage of growing from a single root system: *cloning* is helpful for quickly colonizing an area, but it does not allow enough diversity for pollination, disease control and other important factors. While cloning is quick and easy, seed production allows diversity. For this reason, there are usually several large clones growing side-by-side within a meadow so that pollen and eggs are near enough for easy pollination.

*family field guide*

While the common name refers to one of the most commonly eaten plants in the world (Corn Flakes, creamed corn, corn-on-the-cob, canned corn, etc...), all parts of this plant are poisonous and should not be eaten!

## SOME YEARS BETTER THAN OTHERS

Some years, many Corn Lily flowers are produced while other years very few plants flower. In years when flower production is low, the groves continue to spread through underground rhizomes. Even in years when flowers do not develop, these plants are easy to identify by their unique leaf and stalk.

**Leaf** The common name refers to the thick leaves which are similar to corn leaves.

**Habitat** Corn Lily often dominates sunny damp meadows.

*family field guide*

# Green Gentian
## (Monument Plant)

photo by National Park Service

## Gentian Family

*Frasera speciosa*

**ROCKY MOUNTAIN RELATIVES**
Fringed, Rose, Star and Parry's Gentians

**EASY IDENTIFICATION**
Light green flowers on a tall stalk or large leaves growing from a center point with no flower stalk; grow in sunny montane and subalpine meadows

photo by National Park Service

**Flowers** Each flower has four whitish-green petals with purple dots.

**LIFE CYCLE** Green Gentian has a mysterious life cycle. It grows as a cluster of leaves for years or decades (up to 80 years) before it produces a flower. Scientists are unsure what triggers the flower stalk, but once the plant has stored the right amount of energy and the seasonal conditions are just right, a six-foot tall stalk grows from the leaves and is covered with dozens of greenish flowers. As with Mullein, Alpine Sunflower and Scarlet Gilia, once the flowers are produced and pollination has occurred, the plant dies.

**SEASON-TO-SEASON** The number of Green Gentian flowers spikes every 2-4 years. The number of blooming plants in 2003 was the largest bloom cycle in over 40 years according to scientists at the Rocky Mountain Biological Laboratory in Gothic, Colorado. The number of blooms in 2005 was also very impressive, then, in 2006, a hiker had to explore many miles to find a single plant in bloom. Scientists are not sure what causes the flowering cycle.

**SLOW GROWING STALK** Scientists have discovered that Green Gentian flower stalks begin growing so slowly that they remain microscopic for three years, then, suddenly, grow up to six-feet tall within a month. The tall stalks dry up in fall and remain standing through winter. When the snow melts again in spring, the dried stalks litter the sunny meadows where they blossomed the previous summer.

*family field guide*

**SUNNY AND WARM**

Green Gentian grows best in sunny, open meadows.

**ROSETTE**

The cluster of leaves growing out from a center point is called a rosette. Green Gentian grow a rosette of leaves for decades before the flower salk erupts.

**Leaves** Green Gentian grows as a cluster of leaves for decades before the flower stalk grows.

photo by National Park Service

**Flower** In its final summer before it dies, a flower stalk grows up to six feet tall.

family field guide

# Horsetail
## (Common Horsetail)

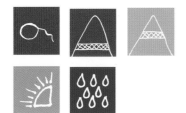

# Horsetail Family

## Equisiteum arvense

### ROCKY MOUNTAIN RELATIVES
Northern and Smooth Scouring Rush

### EASY IDENTIFICATION
Feathery strands grow from a central stalk; grow in wet, shaded areas

**Spores** Horsetail does not produce flowers! Instead, spores grow in spring.

**ANCIENT PLANTS** The earliest Horsetails grew over 300 million years ago and were over 50 feet tall. These early plants looked similar to those in the Rocky Mountains today, but instead of growing as tall as your knees, they grew taller than most buildings.

**GROWING UNDERGROUND** Horsetail and its close relative Scouring Rush spread quickly in wet areas. Underground stems called *rhizomes* can extend seven feet or more from a parent plant with many new plants growing up from the same roots.

**NO FLOWERS, NO SEEDS** Horsetails, mosses and other ancient plants do not form flowers or seeds. Instead of seeds, they make spores. Some spores have female cells (like eggs in flowering plants) and others have male cells (like pollen on flowering plants). The spores drop into water, join together and begin growing a new plant without ever making a seed. Because these plants depend on water instead of insects to make new plants, they have no need for bright-colored flowers or sweet-smelling nectar.

**ONE PLANT, MANY USES** Horsetail and Scouring Rush are both very gritty. Stories say that Indians used these plants to polish pipes, bows and arrows and that early European settlers used them to clean pots and pans and to sand furniture. Both plants contain a mineral called silicon. Silicon is the basic ingredient in glass and makes the gritty texture.

*family field guide*

## DINOSAURS

The first Horsetails grew during the time of dinosaurs over 60,000,000 years ago!

## SCOURING RUSH

## COMMON HORSETAIL

## CLOSE COUSINS

Common Horsetail (right) and Scouring Rush (left) are both in the Horsetail family. They both grow in shady, wet areas, they both grow from spores rather than seeds and they both produce fertile "cones" which produce the spores rather than flowers. While they often grow side by side and have similar characteristics, they are uniquely different plants.

## NOT TOO TASTY

Most animals do not eat Horsetail, but in Fall, when bears eat everything they can get their paws on, they eat it in small amounts. Elk occasionally eat Scouring Rush.

**Neighbors** Horsetail commonly grows next to Scouring Rush in wet, shady areas.

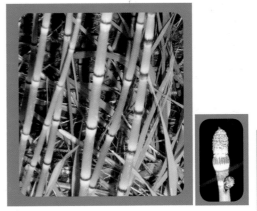

**Scouring Rush** This relative to Horsetail grows hollow segments and also produces spores.

family field guide

# Bistort
## (American Bistort)

## Buckwheat Family
### Polygonum bistortoides

**ROCKY MOUNTAIN RELATIVES**
Alpine Bistort, Sulfur Flower, Curly Dock

**EASY IDENTIFICATION**
Small white flower tufts grow atop a long stem with tiny leaves; grow in sunny subalpine and alpine meadows

**Flower** Dozens of tiny white flowers are clustered like a Q-Tip at the top of the stem.

**ROOT NAMES** The name Bistort refers to the twisted root which curves and curls like an earthworm. Though it does not grow deep, it can curl several feet from the base of this small flower. The root can be as thick as a pencil which is quite large compared to the delicate plant above ground. These roots are used for medicinal treatments that help stop bleeding. They can be made into teas to stop internal bleeding or placed directly on wounds to stop external bleeding.

**UNUSUALLY TALL** Most flowers in the alpine tundra protect themselves from gusty winds by growing low to the ground, or growing hairs on their leaves. Bistort, however, grows shin-high on a thin stem that blows wildly in the wind without any apparent protection. While the stem grows tall, the leaves grow low to the ground and are protected by surrounding grasses. By growing taller than other plants, the flower is able to attract bees, flies and other pollinators from a greater distance than shorter alpine flowers. The strong, tangled roots described above hold the plant in the soil while it gets battered by the wind.

**TRAIL FOOD** The flowers, leaves and stems are eaten by elk, deer and pika and bears eat the roots. Some hikers pop the flowers off and eat them, but the texture is very gritty.

*family field guide*

## TWO TYPES

Two different types of Bistort grow in the alpine meadows. American Bistort appears like a Q-tip with a round, bushy cluster of flowers at the top of its stem (pictured here). Alpine Bistort is shorter and grows a longer series of flowers along the top several inches of its stem.

## BUCKWHEAT FAMILY

Many plants in this family are used for food or medicine. Buckwheat and Rhubarb are the most commonly known plants in this family.

## PERENNIAL

Almost all plants in the alpine tundra are *perennials* which means that they grow back each year. In this high elevation where plants only have 2-3 months to grow each summer, they require more than one season to mature and, in some cases, to produce flowers. If plants at these high elevations were to die each winter, like many plants at lower elevations, they would not have time to germinate, spread their roots, develop flowers and spread their seeds before winter weather moved in.

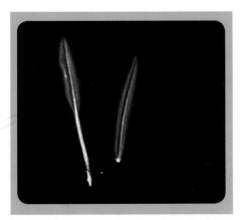

**Leaf** The leaves are small and hardly noticeable as they blend into the grasses.

**Habitat** Bistort is most noticeable in sunny subalpine and alpine meadows.

# Cow Parsnip

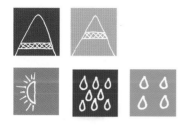

## Parsley Family

*Heracleum sphondilium*

**ROCKY MOUNTAIN RELATIVES**
Angelica, Hemlock Parsley, Poison Hemlock, Mountain Parsley

**EASY IDENTIFICATION**
Huge leaves larger than a dinner plate

**Leaf** The huge leaves are the best way to identify this plant from other similar flowers.

**UMBRELLA OF FLOWERS** Cow Parsnip is very easy to identify by its enormous leaves. In July and August these huge leaves are overshadowed by their beautiful umbrella of white flowers. This pattern of flowers growing in an umbrella-shape is called an *umbel* of flowers. A single Cow Parsnip umbel contains hundreds of tiny flowers all growing from a single stem.

**NAME** The genus name Heracleum is for Hercules. A close relative has the species name *maximum* which tells the story of its size. Cow Parsnip leaves are larger than a computer screen (up to 24 inches wide), their stems can grow taller than most adults (up to 7 feet tall) and their flower umbels grow as large as an adult's head (up to 1 foot around).

**COMPANION PLANTS** These giants grow along streambanks, in sunny meadows and beneath Aspen groves. In late July and August, when Cow Parsnip and its most common companion Larkspur, are both in bloom, they create a spectacular display beneath the trembling aspen leaves.

**PARSLEY FAMILY** This plant family includes such familiar members as carrots, celery, dill, fennel, parsley and parsnip. Not all species, however, are edible. The great philosopher Socrates was sentenced to die by drinking a potion of Poison Hemlock, a close relative. Several species of Hemlock grow in this region so never eat any of these similar-looking plants.

*family field guide*

## BETTER SAFE THAN SORRY

The flowers of several close relatives, Poison Hemlock and Water Hemlock, both grow in the Rocky Mountain region and can cause serious illness or even death. Their flowers look very similar to those of Cow Parsnip. Be safe wtih all of these plants; never put the leaves, stalks or roots in your mouth for any reason.

## COMMON FLOWER

The flowers of Angelica, Osha and several species of Hemlock all look very similar to Cow Parsnip. The best way to identify Cow Parsnip is by the leaves.

## STEMMED FLUTES

The hollow stems of many plants in this family are often used as toys for children. Play carefully; Poison Hemlock has similar flowers and can cause serious illness!

**Flowers** The umbrella-shaped flower clusters are similar to other flowers in the region.

**Habitat** Cow Parsnip grows in aspen groves and along streambanks in moist soil.

# Geranium
## (White and Sticky Geranium)

## Geranium Family

*Geranium richardsonii (white)*
*Geranium viscossissimum (sticky)*

**ROCKY MOUNTAIN RELATIVES**
Cranesbill

**EASY IDENTIFICATION**
Five-petaled pink or white flower; leaves are similar to poisonous Larkspur and Monkshood and are not a good identifier

**Flowers** Both types of Geranium flowers have five petals with pink veins.

**THEY'RE EVERYWHERE** Geranium is a very common plant in montane and subalpine ecosystems. They grow in partly-shaded, damp forests and can be found in aspen groves, riverbanks, streambeds, sunny openings within evergreen forests and just about anywhere they can keep their roots wet. Though the flowers are small and delicate, the plants are often very bushy and grow waist-high.

**TWO TYPES** White Geranium and Sticky Geranium look very similar. Sticky Geranium is bright pink with bright pink veins in the flower petals. White Geranium ranges from pure white to slightly pink with similarly colored veins in the petals. These veins act as "nectar guides" to pollinating insects because they lead the insects toward the center of the plant where nectar is located. The nectar guides in geraniums reflect ultraviolet light which humans cannot see. This extra light reflection, makes the veins especially attractive to bees whose eyes can detect the reflection.

**CATAPULT** After the flower is pollinated, the seed capsules begin to curl upward but remain attached at their base. As the pressure from the expanding seed capsules builds then breaks, the seeds are catapulted into the air, shooting several yards away from the parent plant. Therefore they do not depend on animals or wind to disperse their seeds.

*family field guide*

## DIFFERENT LOOK

The delicate wild Geranium flowers look very different from the huge flowers of their domestic cousins. The huge flowers of garden Geraniums are favorites of gardeners. These colorful cousins are *annuals* which need to be planted each year. Perennial Geraniums which look very similar to these delicate wildflowers are also available at garden centers.

## COMMON LEAF

Geranium leaves look very similar to Larkspur and Monkshood and all grow in similar conditions. Geranium leaves, however, turn bright red in fall.

## BIG AND BUSHY

These plants grow in bunches up to three feet tall and can have dozens of flowers in bloom at one time.

**Leaves** The leaves are as large as a third grader's hand and turn red in fall.

**Flower** Colors vary from pure white to pink in White Geranium and are bright pink in Sticky Geranium

family field guide

# Mariposa Lily
## (Sego Lily)

# Lily Family

*Calochortus gunnisonii*

**ROCKY MOUNTAIN RELATIVES**
Corn Lily, False Solomon Seal, Glacier Lily

**EASY IDENTIFICATION**
Unique flower on top of a single long stem; grow in sunny meadows

**Leaves** The leaves are very small, which helps them hold onto water in dry conditions.

**NAMES** The genus name *Calochortus* means "beautiful" in Greek. Spanish explorers later called this plant *Mariposa*, Spanish for "butterfly," perhaps for the delicate wing-like petals or the detailed coloring in the plant's center. The Shoshone Indian word *Sego* means "edible bulb" referring to the walnut-sized root structures which taste like potato. The species name *gunnisonii* is in honor of the explorer Captain J.W. Gunnison who explored modern-day Colorado and Utah.

**UTAH STATE FLOWER** Three species of Sego Lily occur in Colorado. The one pictured above (*gunisonii*) has hundreds of yellow "hairs" in its center and is the most common in mountain regions. The other two species are more common in dry, rocky canyons. Sego Lily is the state flower of Utah where these dry canyon environments are common. Ironically, Captain Gunnison and his expedition were all murdered in Utah.

**SMALL LEAVES** Water moves from the roots, to the stem, to the leaves and is used by all parts of the plant along the way. Water exits the plant through the leaves; this is called *transpiration*. Very hot temperatures speed up transpiration, pulling the water out from the leaves faster than the plant can use it. The small leaves along the stem provide a very small surface from which the water can evaporate, allowing the delicate plant to hold and use water more efficiently.

*family field guide*

## SUN LOVER

This flower loves full sun and dry conditions. It may be found in sunny sage flats in the lowlands, sunny montane meadows or in aspen groves.

## DROUGHT RESISTANT

Mariposa Lily is designed for dry conditions. It grows tall so that butterflies can see it standing among tall grasses, but it is very thin. With only 1-2 leaves per plant, water does not easily evaporate from the tiny leaves. Blue Flax and Scarlet Gilia, both plants that grow in the hot, dry conditins, have similarly small leaves.

**Seeds** After the flower has been pollinated a seed pod forms.

**Stem** Mariposa Lily forms a delicate flower at the top of a single, long stem.

family field guide

# Yarrow

## Sunflower Family

*Achilles millefolium*

**ROCKY MOUNTAIN RELATIVES**
Daisies, asters, sunflowers, sages, thistles

**EASY IDENTIFICATION**
Feathery leaves; clusters of flattened white flowers

**Flower** Yarrow flowers grow shin-high along a delicate stem.

**IT'S EVERYWHERE** Yarrow grows in sunny meadows, dry hillsides and aspen groves from lowlands to alpine meadows. Plants are most commonly produced from *rhizomes*, underground stems which spread from the parent plant, then grow new plants above ground nearby. Because these plants grow and reproduce quickly in sunny meadows, they are some of the first flowers to grow following fires and avalanches. These same characteristics that make them good *pioneers* in newly burned areas, allow them to dominate a garden, so plant them cautiously.

**NAME** The genus name *Achilles* refers to the Greek hero who used the plant to treat his army's wounds in battle. Yarrow leaves are known to stop bleeding; if you have a bloody nose, chew a yarrow leaf then stick it up your nostril! The species name *millefolium* means "a thousand leaves" and refers to the fern-like leaves which appear as thousands of tiny leaflets.

**VERY COMMON** Yarrow is one of the most common plants in the Rocky Mountains. It grows in all life zones, moist aspen groves, dry meadows and sun-baked roadbeds. It's flowers bloom from June through September and even if you don't notice the flowers, look carefully in any grassy meadow for mats of their fern-like leaves waiting to form a flower in coming years.

*family field guide*

## WILDLIFE FOOD

These common flowers are a favorite food for wildlife including deer, bighorn sheep, pocket gopher and marmot.

## PIONEER

Because this plant grows well in full sun and spreads quickly through underground *rhizomes*, Yarrow is one of the first plants to grow after disturbances including fire, avalanche and construction. Plants that are the first to grow into unvegetated hillsides are called *pioneer species.*

## DROUGHT RESISTANT

Yarrow can survive long droughts because they have sturdy roots which can extend over a foot into the soil and their tiny leaflets do not allow water to evaporate.

**Leaves** The fern-like leaves are the easiest way to identify this plant.

**Habitat** Yarrow grows in a tangle of grasses and other sun-loving plants.

*family field guide*

# Photo Comparisons

## CONE COMPARISONS

**Blue Spruce**
(larger than Engelmann Spruce)

**Engelmann Spruce**
(smaller than Blue Spruce)

**Ponderosa Pine**
(the largest of all Rocky Mountain cones)

photo by JNational Park Service

**Subalpine Fir**
(stands upright and does not drop)

**Lodgepole**
(serotinous cone)

**Douglas Fir**

**Pinyon Pine**

**Juniper**

family field guide

## LEAF COMPARISONS

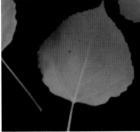

**Heart-shaped** (Aspen)

**Lobed** (Gambel Oak)

**Lanceolate** (Willow)

**Toothed** (Arnica)

**Opposite** (Monkeyflower)

**Radial** (Lupine)

## BERRY COMPARISONS

Chokecherry

Raspberry

Serviceberry

Dogwood

Elderberry

Wild Rose (rose hip)

# FLOWER COMPARISONS

Arnica

Arrowleaf Balsamroot

Cinquefoil

Dandelion

Glacier Lily

Monkeyflower

Mullein

Alpine Sunflower

Oregon Grape

Iris

Larkspur

Lupine

Monkshood

Silky Phacelia

Sky Pilot

Blue Flax

Bluebells

Columbine

Clover

Elephant-head

*family field guide*

Fairyslipper

Fireweed

Parry's Primrose

Moss Campion

Thistle

Rose

Paintbrush

Red Columbine

King's Crown

Scarlet Gilia

Cattail

Corn Lily

Green Gentian

Cow Parsnip

Geranium

Mariposa Lily

Bistort

Dogwood

Yarrow

Serviceberry

Chokecherry

# Glossary

**Acidic** An unfavorable condition to most living things where extra hydrogen creates a pH less than seven.

**Annual** A plant that dies after one year of growth.

**Anther** The male part of a plant that carries pollen.

**Botany** The technical name for the study of plants.

**Botanist** A scientist who studies plants.

**Bulb** A short underground stem, with many fleshy scale-like leaves filled with food

**Cambium** A layer of cells between the bark and the wood of a tree where new growth occurs.

**Carbohydrates** Sugars and starches that are the most efficient source of food energy; produced by plants.

**Catkin** A cluster of tiny flowers, usually fuzzy and caterpillar-shaped, often drooping on willows, birches and other deciduous plants.

**Chlorophyll** The green pigment in plants that captures energy from the sun for photosynthesis.

**Chloroplasts** The cells in leaves which contains chlorophyll.

**Clone** A group of identical plants (or cells, genes or organisms) that originate from a single parent.

**Coevolution** The process by which two or more organisms develop specialized traits and characteristics in accordance with the other. Species which have coevolved usually depend on each other for survival.

**Common Name** The name or names by which a plant is commonly known.

**Companion Plants** Plants that often grow together in the same habitat.

**Duff** A layer of leaves, dried needles and decaying material on the forest floor.

**Feeding Tree** A tree used by animals for food.

**Fertilized** The touching of male cells and female cells which produces the growth of a new seed.

**Fruit** A ripe ovary which protects and nourishes the seeds within.

**Germinate** When a seed begins to sprout, usually in the presence of water and proper temperatures.

**Hardy** Plants able to survive extreme conditions.

**Hemiparasite** A plant that gets its energy from photosynthesis and from other plants.

**Hybrid** The offspring of two different species or two different genera (plural for genus).

**Indicator Species** A species whose characteristics show the presence of specific environmental conditions and are representative of a certain habitat type or function.

**Introduced Species** A species of plant or animal brought from one place to a new place where it never existed before; non-native.

**Invasive Species** A species that has moved into an area and reproduced so aggressively that it has replaced some of the original plant species.

**Leaflet** Small leaf parts growing from a single stem; many leaflets combine to form a compund leaf.

**Lenticel** A round or long bump on the bark of woody stems and roots that functions as a breathing pore.

**Lobed** A leaf shape with curved or rounded edges.

**Moss** Small, leafy plants that do not produce flowers or seeds.

**Mutualistic** An association between two different species in which each member benefits.

**Microhabitat** A small area where an organism lives that has different conditions from other areas that might be right next door.

**Native Species** A species of plant or animal that occurs naturally in an area.

**Non-native Species** A species of plant or animal brought from one place to a new place where it never existed before; introduced species.

**Ovary** The round part of the female part of the plant which holds the female cells (eggs). When the male cells land in the ovary and touch the eggs, new seeds are formed in the ovary.

**Photosynthesis** The process of using energy from sunlight along with water and carbon dioxide to make carbohydrates (sugars) and oxygen.

**Perennial** A plant that lives for more than 2 growing seasons.

**Pioneer Species** The first plant species to grow into a disturbed area.

**Pistil** The female parts of a flower consisting of an ovary, style and stigma.

**Pollen** The male plant cells.

**Pollination** The process of carrying pollen to the eggs to create a new seed.

**Potandry** A plant behavior in which blossoms of the same plant open at different times.

**Rhizomes** Underground, creeping stems which form new plants.

**Root Sucker** A new plant which grows up from the roots of a parent tree.

**Scientific Name** The Latin name given to an organism so that it is recognizable in all languages.

**Scree Field** A field of relatively small rocks no larger than a dinner plate.

**Sepal** One of the outermost circle of leaves surrounding the reproductive organs of a flower; usually green.

**Sertinous Cone** A pine cone that requires heat from a fire to open and release the seed.

**Stomata** Tiny holes on the leaves which open and close to allow gases to move in and out of the plant.

**Succession** The gradual process of change in an ecosystem by the replacement of one community by another.

**Succulent** A plant that has a specialized fleshy tissue in roots, stems, or leaves for the conservation of water.

**Talus Slopes** Talus slopes are more angled than a scree slope. Talus rocks are also larger than scree.

**Toothed** A leaf with a jagged edge.

**Transpiration** The process of water moving out of the plant through the leaves.

**Umbel** A branched flower structure resembling an (upside-down) umbrella.

**Vegetative Reproduction** The production of new plants from sources other than a seed (rhizomes, root suckers, cuttings, etc.)

# Index

*family field guide*

# References

Corner, E.J.H. 1964. *The Life of Plants*. University of Chicago Press.

Duft, Joseph F.; Moseley, Robert K. 1989. *Alpine Wildflowers of the Rocky Mountains*. Mountain Press Publishing Company.

Ells, James. 2006. *Rocky Mountain Flora*. The Colorado Mountain Club Press.

Fielder, John. 1994. *Wildflowers of Colorado*. Westcliffe Publishers, Inc.

Guennel, G.K. 1995. *Guide to Colorado Wildflowers: Volume 1 Plains & Foothills*. Westcliffe Publishers, Inc.

Guennel, G.K. 1995. *Guide to Colorado Wildflowers: Volume 2 Mountains*. Westcliffe Publishers, Inc.

Huggins, Janis Lindsey. 2004. *Wild At Heart: A Natural History Guide Dedicated to Snowmass, Aspen and the Maroon Bells Wilderness*. The Town of Snowmass Village.

Lerner, Carol. 1989. *Plant Families*. Morrow Junior Books

Little, Elbert Luther. 1980. *The Audubon Society Field Guide to North American Trees, Western Region*. Knopf.

Munger, Susan H. 2003. *Common to This Country: Botanical Discoveries of Lewis and Clark*. Artisan.

Raven, Peter H.; Evert, Ray F.; Curtis, Helena. 1971. *Biology of Plants*. Worth Publishers, Inc.

Spellenberg, Richard. 2001. *The Audubon Society Field Guide to North American Wildflowers, Western Region*. Knopf.

US Postal Service. 1992. *Wildflowers: A Collection of U.S. Commemorative Stamps*.

Zwinger, Ann H.; Willard, Beatrice E. 1996. *Land Above the Trees: A Guide to American Alpine Tundra*. Johnson Printing.

## About the Author

As a third and fourth grader, Garrick spent most of his outdoor hours on soccer fields and basketball courts, but also climbing Cottonwoods along the Highline Canal in Littleton, CO. More recently, Garrick taught environmental education at the Aspen Center for Environmental Studies for four years, taught high school science in the African kingdom of Lesotho for two years and taught third and fourth grades at the Aspen Community School for three years. He lives with his wife, Lindsay, and their son Mason in Basalt, CO. He has written two other books: *Family Field Guide Series Volume 1: Rocky Mountain Mammals* and *Mountain Biking: Aspen to Glenwood*.

## About the Illustrator

Hilary is an artist, a naturalist, and an educator. Some of her earliest memories are of wearing smocks and painting at easels in pre-school in West Lafayette, IN. Her passion for the visual arts has been lifelong. She is an illustrator and mixed media artist who has worked in photography, oil painting, textiles, printmaking and papermaking. She sells enameled jewelry with bold colors and geometric designs. In addition, she works in the field of scientific illustration. Hilary has been an educator for the past ten years. With degrees in both biology and art education she has taught environmental education, guided adventure trips and taught visual arts at the K-12 level. She has been teaching art to K-8th grade students at the Aspen Communtiy School since 2003. She also teaches at Anderson Ranch during the summer. She has illustrated one other book: *Family Field Guide Series Volume 1: Rocky Mountain Mammals.* Hilary lives in Aspen, CO.

## field notes